AUTHORS:
Eileen Beamish, Social Research Centre Ltd
Donal McDade, Social Market Research Ltd
Maurice Mulvenna, Suzanne Martin, TRAIL Living Lab, University of Ulster
Dia Soilemezi, University of Portsmouth

We wish to acknowledge the contribution to this book, including editing, by
Fiona McMahon, School of Communication, University of Ulster,
Tara Dean & Amy Drahota, University of Portsmouth
Jonathan Wallace & Brendan Galbraith, TRAIL Living Lab, University of Ulster

Special thanks to our graphic designer, Dani McFerran

SUPPORTED BY:
HEIF, ENoLL, EU Commission, PARTERRE Project, University of Ulster, University of Portsmouth.

PUBLISHED BY: TRAIL Living Lab, University of Ulster

PREFACE
BEFORE STARTING

Professor Maurice Mulvenna
TRAIL Living Lab
MARCH 2012

In the University of Ulster, we've been working with people to help direct our research and innovation activities for many years. We recognise the value of engaging with people and how it can make the engagement much more rewarding and valuable in terms of research contributions. It's also more fun!

We established TRAIL (Translating Research And Innovation Lab) to support our research and innovation activities across several key research disciplines including business, information & communication technologies, occupational therapy, art, health care, media studies research, social care and other disciplines.

When we adopted the concept of Living Labs in 2006, it was a fresh European initiative placing people at the very centre of service and product development and innovation. Living labs involve partnerships between academics, public and private entities, concentrating on the development of new information services, businesses, technologies and markets, with strong involvement of user communities.

TRAIL has been particularly successful in helping engage with ageing people in Northern Ireland, but it also engages with people of all ages, and indeed with many companies and social enterprises to help research and innovate new services and products.

Our vision for engagement is founded on the evidence that providing communities and enterprises with tools at grass roots level to engage people in the creative design of solutions to the problems that they face, often inspires their thinking and results in outcomes that better match their needs.

We wanted to develop a toolkit to help empower other living labs and communities generally to develop their own evidence base to help in decision marking and development of solutions to their local problems. In October 2011, we published the results of the first survey of living labs from across Europe and beyond.

The results of this survey clearly indicated that a majority of living labs found it difficult to engage with people in a constructive way, and to translate engagement with users into new services, solutions and products. A majority also said that they would benefit from access to practical advice and assistance on engaging with users.

We developed this toolkit to help anyone currently operating living labs or wishing to carry out research and innovation activities with users to make it easier to translate from user needs to products, services and solutions. We hope that you find it of practical use and do please let us know how it can be improved by emailing us at trail@ulster.ac.uk.

FOREWORD
TO THIS TOOLKIT

Professor Àlvaro Oliveira
*President of the ENoLL Association
and Chair of the Council*
EUROPEAN NETWORK OF LIVING LABS (ENOLL)

The Living Lab movement is emerging globally as a tool for economic and social development at the local and regional scale, providing significant opportunities for rural, urban and regional development, both to large companies and to Small-to-Medium-Enterprise (SME) innovation, leveraging their sustainable competitiveness, and giving a new role for public authorities in promoting and facilitating innovation. Thus, today the Living Labs are a widely recognised and accepted pillar of the European Innovation System.

European Living Labs have evolved over the past seven years based on and strongly interlinked with national and European Policy and Innovation initiatives in the broad thematic areas:

- Energy Efficiency
  Sustainable Energy
  Climate change
- Well Being and Health
- Smart Cities
  Future Internet
  Internet of things
- Social Innovation
  Social Inclusion
- e-Government
  e-Participation
- Creative Media
  User driven contents
  Social Networks
  Web 2.0
- Thematic Tourism
  Culture Services
- Territorial and rural development
- Sustainable Mobility
- Industrial and logistics development.
- Security

The European Commission has supported the Living Labs growth from the outset, recognising that user-driven open innovation is an efficient way to deal with market fragmentation and obstacles, making the innovation process more efficient by bridging the gap between Research, Development and Innovation (RDI) and market entrance and supporting better and faster take-up of RDI results.

These methodologies are rapidly becoming the new mainstream method of innovating as they enable SMEs to create lead markets by overcoming existing barriers in local and regional markets in Europe.

The Living Labs model includes citizen participation from the very outset of the creative process of technology development.

As a result, evaluating aspects such as social and economic implications of new technologies has become more accurate. So the needs of users are better listened to and fulfilled. With Living Labs the development of technologies and creation of innovations steps out from closed laboratories, into everyday life.

A first turning point came with the Helsinki Manifesto launched by the Finnish EU Presidency in December 2006, which established the European Network of Living Labs (ENoLL) as "an important step towards a new European innovation infrastructure".

With the solid support of the initial structure of 19 Living Labs, Living Labs have together formed an umbrella organization called the European Network of Living Labs, a non-profit association with the overall aim to exploit synergies between the network members in terms of networking, sharing good practices, provision of services and tools and the ability to access different user communities.

The community has grown through 5 yearly 'waves' of membership to 274 Living Labs of which 36 are outside of Europe, covering six Continents. National Living Lab networks have been established in several Member States and regional networks in China, Latin America, and Africa.

Each Living Lab brings different groups and sectorial associations into its partnership, involving often hundreds of SMEs in its activities and leading to the estimated 25,000 organisations affected by ENoLL activities overall.

Following a strategy of globalisation of the Living Labs movement, ENoLL has concluded several strategic Memorandum of Understanding (MoUs) with organisations such as the Beijing City Administration Information System and Equipment Center (CAISEC), Ubiquitous Network Industry and the Technology Development Forum

(UNITED, the Chinese Future Internet and Internet of Things initiative), the Food and Agricultural Organisation of United Nations (FAO), LLiSA (Living Labs in Southern Africa), Asian Smart Living Summer School and more recently with the World Bank.

Through these MoUs, ENoLL is building a portfolio of activities, initiatives, exchanges, and pilot experiments throughout the world, building international networks and offering exceptional opportunities to European SMEs and the broader EU RDI community.

Despite all of the achievements of the community, there are still many challenges ahead of us. For example we need more information on understanding the user experience, breaking down the complexity of Living Labs infrastructures and activities, the overall governance of open ecosystems, including issues such as Intellectual Property Rights (IPR), privacy and responsibility, etc. and evaluation and impact assessment of Living Labs.

To this end, we need guidelines such as the TRAIL User Participation Toolkit for Living Labs. I am grateful to the TRAIL Living Lab, an active ENoLL member, for whose path finding work in the area of user participation underpins the toolkit you are holding in your hands. They have used their in-depth experience to create these reader-friendly guidelines that can be used by existing as well as emerging Living Labs in Europe and beyond. We hope that this toolkit will give Living Lab professionals greater insight into the processes and tools they need to put in place.

The European Network of Living Labs is delighted to support the diffusion of the toolkit towards its members. I encourage you to use this Toolkit and to accelerate the use of Living Labs methodology development towards developing a more sustainable society.

CONTENTS

1.0
INTRODUCTION
TO USER PARTICIPATION

BEING USER-CENTRED SAVES TIME AND MONEY IN THE LONG RUN.
IT CAN ALSO PRODUCE BETTER PRODUCTS AND SERVICES.

In this chapter we will discuss:
• What is means to be 'user-centred';
• Why being user-centred is a good idea;
• What user participation actually is;
• How it is structured;
• The principles and values that, when observed, greatly enhance the effectiveness and quality of user participation.

1.1 WHAT DOES IT MEAN TO BE 'USER-CENTRED'?

What is 'user participation', 'user involvement', 'user engagement', who is a 'user'? It may also help just to note that definitions of 'user involvement' may vary from country to country and from discipline to discipline.

Definitions of Public and Patient Involvement – refer to http://www.invo.org.uk/About_Us.asp

1.2 TEN GOOD REASONS TO BE USER-CENTRED

ONE
Users can have good ideas. Twenty five years of research has shown that users, rather than manufacturers, are often the initial developers of what later becomes commercially significant products.

TWO
Users understand needs. Trying to understand what users really need is highly complex. If you only use conventional market research techniques you will only get so far.

THREE:
Manufacturers and service providers gain from user insights. The user perspective, is typically focused on critical factors such as 'Does this actually work?', 'What are the drawbacks?', 'How significant are these?' The answers that ensue can help a manufacturer avoid investing significant sums of money in products or services that are unlikely to meet the needs of the market – it's a 'win-win' situation.

FOUR
There will be no need to 'second guess' the problem or issues around the solution; you can gain greater understanding by involving the users directly with your project.

FIVE
As developers of products, services, solutions, you may gain a greater sense of esteem and sense of value in the work you are undertaking, as you will feel more assured about the integrity and future applicability of the work.

SIX
The work you are undertaking is more likely to be beneficial for users if they are informing what you are doing. Ideas and solutions can be tailored to the unmet needs and market gaps of the population of interest.

SEVEN
The chances for successful or increased take-up of the product, device, or service you are developing will be improved because you have taken the needs of the users into consideration.

EIGHT
Users may feel more satisfied as they know they've been involved in the process and informed the final product. Users may feel more valued and listened to, as opposed to simply being considered as 'consumers'.

NINE
In the long-run, it is possible that user-involvement may save you time and money by limiting the number of 'wrong turns' which could be made, which would result in having to go back and start again.

TEN
There are moral, ethical and rights reasons. A strong case can be made that the public should be actively involved in any publicly funded research which may impact on their health status, for example.

1.3 WHAT IS 'USER PARTICIPATION'?

" 'User participation'describes a series of methods and processes that are specifically designed to actively involve people in influencing decisions that shape policies, practices, products or services." [2]

[2] Source: Social Research Centre, 2011.

The term 'user participation' has lots of academic definitions but it really about people and involving people in decision-making processes, whether at local level or at national and international levels. People want to give their views and do feel better if they are involved - whatever the decision-making process is about.

Being 'involved' also has a dynamic of its own in the process of participating in decision-making. People have the opportunity to speak their mind, listen to what others are saying, and generally explore how their views are perceived by others, and how they perceive the opinions of others.

At its simplest, user participation is a meeting of people with little structure or planning to the organisation of the meeting.

However, it is more common for some structure to be applied to ensure that the viewpoints of all those who attend are accommodated and recorded for sharing after the event. Events can be structured as town hall meetings, offering communities the chance to air issues common at town or village level. They can also be more formal structures in place with sophisticated methods of recording using video and audio.

More recently, user participation is also taking place through social media websites and 'apps' such as Facebook and Twitter offering access to extremely large numbers of people via electronic channels. These can provide completely new paradigms of interaction; for example, 'crowd sourcing' solutions to community problems.

1.4 USER PARTICIPATION - THE BASIC PROCESS

There are a variety of reasons why organisations involve users (See ten reasons earlier in this chapter).

If you follow a user-centred approach, you are primarily involving users to try to understand:

- **Knowledge**
  What they know or don't know about your product or service;

- **Attitudes**
  How they perceive your product or service and why;

- **Behaviour**
  How they currently interact, will interact or don't interact with your product or service.

Whenever you involve users, you are essentially entering into a process which has a beginning, a middle and an end . You can think of this as three stages:

- **Before** participation;
- **During** participation; and,
- **After** participation.

These processes involve you asking yourself, (or your team, or your organisation etc), a series of questions as follows:

Before participation:

- **Rationale**
  Why are we doing this? For what purpose?

- **Objectives**
  What are we trying to find out?

- **Existing knowledge**
  What do we already know?

- **Who**
  Who will we ask/involve?

During participation:

- **Approach**
  How will we go about involving users?

- **Quality check**
  Has our user participation been good enough? How will we know?

After participation:

- **Findings**
  What does all the feedback from users tell us?

- **Implications**
  What does this feedback mean for our proposed service/product?

- **Feeding back**
  How will we share our findings and conclusions with users?

What's important about what you have just read?

The key to organising user participation is...

Understanding the basic process well in advance.
This helps you prepare for every aspect of the exercise, understand what is needed at each stage, and helps you understand how to manage your findings.

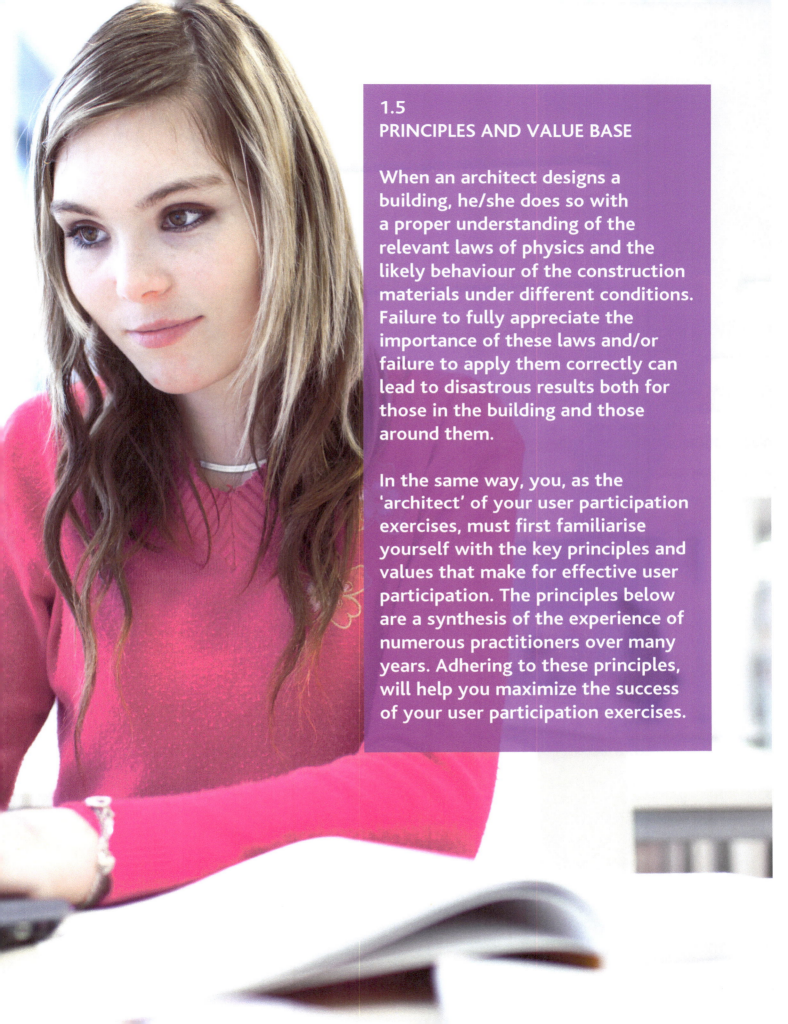

1.5
PRINCIPLES AND VALUE BASE

When an architect designs a building, he/she does so with a proper understanding of the relevant laws of physics and the likely behaviour of the construction materials under different conditions. Failure to fully appreciate the importance of these laws and/or failure to apply them correctly can lead to disastrous results both for those in the building and those around them.

In the same way, you, as the 'architect' of your user participation exercises, must first familiarise yourself with the key principles and values that make for effective user participation. The principles below are a synthesis of the experience of numerous practitioners over many years. Adhering to these principles, will help you maximize the success of your user participation exercises.

Use consultation methods that are appropriate to the needs of users and will yield information which is valid and reliable. This often means using more than one approach to participation, giving a more robust and reliable outcome.

1.5.1
BEFORE PARTICIPATION

Honest intention
Participation exercises must have an honest intention. Be willing to listen to the views advanced by users, and be prepared to be influenced when making subsequent decisions.

Visible commitment
Demonstrate a clear corporate commitment to involving users consistently and equitably.

Clarity of purpose
Have genuine reasons for seeking feedback and communicate these clearly.

User identification and engagement
Identify the relevant users. Inform them about the purpose and boundaries of the participation exercise and explain how the outcomes will be used. For example, contact the users directly by email, letter, or create a poster to explain the purpose of your project. Sometimes it is advisable to contact the "gatekeepers" who can put you in contact with more users.

Clarity of process
Ensure that the way in which you propose to use the feedback given to you by users (i.e. in terms of how it will be analysed and the results shared with others) is understood by the participants. Also, explain what you intend to do with your findings. Make sure that their expectations meet your own expectations.

Proportionality
Ensure that the inputs to participation exercises (financial, staff, users' time etc.) are commensurate with the potential impacts of the participation exercise.

Efficiency
Strive to reduce duplication of effort and the burden on users by seeking to join-up participation exercises within your own organisation and across partner organisations wherever possible.

Policy compliance
Ensure that the overall design and conduct of the consultation is compliant with all of your organisation's relevant policies e.g. interaction with vulnerable adults, child protection, physical accessibility, data protection and confidentiality etc.

Practicalities
Arrange a time and place convenient to participants. Central locations, with parking or nearby bus/train stops, disabled access/toilet are preferred. Is it easier for them to travel to you or for you to visit them? Offer them the choice if possible. Make sure participants are comfortable and feel safe. Offer them refreshments and also to pay any travelling expenses. If you are also intending to access participants who have specific experiences and knowledge you wish to engage with, you may need to consider their specific requirements.

For example, if you wish to target parents of young children (e.g. under five) you may need to consider child care arrangements. Do you consider running a crèche whilst the parents meet with you or do you offer to pay the parents for other child care?

Organising your project
Design your participation exercise depending on your resources and time. Make sure your team is well trained and you have all your required materials.

Prepare all the forms and check your equipment, i.e. voice recorders.

Steering Committee
Create partnerships among all key stakeholder groups and invite them to sit on your Steering Committee as they can advise you on many aspects of user involvement.

1.5.2
DURING PARTICIPATION

Timing
Seek to conduct participation exercises when there are still elements than can truly be influenced by the exercise. The elements which can and cannot be influenced should be clearly identified at the outset so that expectations can be managed appropriately.

Time span
Provide users with adequate time to engage. Encourage participation and invite all users to participate when ready.

Robustness
Use consultation methods that are appropriate to the needs of users and will yield information which is valid and reliable. This often means using more than one approach to participation. Robust results are more likely when two different approaches are applied and the outcomes are the same.

Enabling
Support users with sufficient and accessible information and, wherever possible, access to tools and skills to enable them to give informed feedback to the best of their abilities.

Accessibility & inclusion
Ensure that suitable methods are in place to support those who may be at risk of disadvantage in giving their views. In order to engage with users from ethnic minorities, you may need to translate your materials and arrange for an interpreter to facilitate the communication.

Consenting & Confidentiality

Ask the participants to sign a consent form before the exercise to ensure they understand the information they received and they are happy to take part. People may feel anxious when they sign forms and they may need you to explain more about issues of confidentiality and anonymity. Explain where the data will be stored, for how long and who will have access to it.

1.5.3
AFTER PARTICIPATION

Integrity
Report the findings from the participation exercise in a manner that honours the points made by the users.

Due regard
Whilst other factors may need to be considered, use the findings from participation exercises in the manner explained to/agreed with users at the outset. Keep anonymity and impartiality when analysing and reporting your findings.

Care with 'attribution'
Just because something occurs at the same time as something else is no guarantee that one thing caused the other.

If we think that it is our product or service that is affecting users in a particular way, we need to ensure that (a) we have asked the questions in the correct way and (b) we understand what other factors might be influencing their answers and rule these factors out (as far as possible) or seek to separate them out in some way.

For example, if we were asking users to tell us which service (A or B) they would prefer to use, we need to be sure that the answers they give us relate to, for example, the features of the services and the differences in value that they attribute to those features (if that is what we are interested in learning about).

It is possible that some users may have direct experience of service A and not B and others may have experience of B and not A and the answers they give you may relate more to their level of familiarity and 'comfort' with a particular type of service that the actual merits of service A or B.

Feedback
Notify users about the outcomes of the participation exercise. Show how their contributions were used in the decision-making process. Importantly, if key suggestions they made have not been taken on board, explain why. Send a transcription or summary of results back to participants if they have requested it on the consent form.

Continuous improvement
Carry out a review afterwards to find out what lessons can be learned from the participation process (e.g. whether some aspects of the process were more effective than others). Share the lessons learned as widely as possible.

1.5.4
GENERAL

Empowerment
Conduct participation exercises so that, as far as possible, users experience them as constructive and empowering interactions with you, your organisation etc.

Efficient, effective and economical use of resources
The amount of information you can obtain from your participation exercises will depend, to an extent, on the amount of time and money that can be allocated to them.

Appropriate design, therefore, is crucial. Bearing in mind the important principles of inclusion and equity, the design of participation exercises should always consider how to maximise insight using the least amount of resources (time and money).

One of the key considerations in this is finding out what we already know (which is usually relatively cheap to do) before proceeding with (more expensive) interviews, focus groups or surveys.

Consistency
Ensure that any third parties appointed to carry out participation exercises on your behalf can demonstrate that their approach is compliant with the above best practice principles.

What's important about what you have just read?

Dynamism
User participation is a multi-faceted process. It can generate new ideas, bring light to issues, suggest solutions and enhance the quality of products/services.

Structure
Participation exercises always have a beginning, a middle and an end.

Principles
There are a set of key principles which, when observed, greatly enhance the quality and effectiveness of participation exercises.

2.0
LIVING LABS
AN INTRODUCTION

THE DIRECT INVOLVEMENT OF USERS IN THE
DEVELOPMENT OF ESSENTIAL PRODUCTS AND SERVICES.

In this chapter we will discuss:
• The concept of innovation and user-driven innovation in particular;
• The notion of a 'Living Lab'; and,
• Some of the challenges to the use of 'Living Labs'.

2.1 INNOVATION

Innovation is 'change in the thought process for doing something, or the useful application of new inventions or discoveries'; 'to make changes in something established, especially by introducing new methods, ideas, or products'.

The concept and benefits of user-driven innovation

Historically, innovation has been characterised as a linear process, driven and controlled by the industrial developers of products for the marketplace. In the information society, it is increasingly seen as a catalyst for growth and competitiveness and has been enthusiastically promoted at regional, national and international level and included in new policy formulation.

However, it has evolved from a linear process towards a network model involving partners supporting innovation, often focused on cycles of innovation activity. These partnerships of interaction can take many forms but one model that is increasingly being used is a triple-helix model of engagement where the three types of stakeholders are industry, government and academia, often also called academic-public-private partnerships. This model, and its variants, works well within the concept of network economy, facilitating ad hoc or permanent partnerships as required, focusing on problem-solving and

commercial exploitation of intellectual property and know-how arising from the partnerships. The most interesting facet of these kinds of models for engagement is the active participation of academia, cementing a role for entrepreneurial universities in innovation activities that are becoming increasingly influenced by network economy concepts.

However, arguably the greatest change in how we should consider innovation is coming about in open innovation, where it is claimed that innovation can thrive when a company utilises a network of partnerships beyond its traditional internal resources.

The partnerships can facilitate technology development, licensing of existing intellectual property, access to external capital as well as sales and marketing partnerships. A typology for open innovation is emerging encompassing different strategies, for example, innovation seeker, innovation provider, intermediary and open

innovator. However, while there is a significant volume of academic publishing activity that embraces open innovation as a new paradigm to help describe innovation in our networked knowledge economies, there are also those that assert that open innovation is 'old wine in new bottles'.

Innovation researchers argue that while closed innovation principles are indeed limited, companies today no longer adhere to these closed innovation principles but rather have long ago changed their mindsets to think beyond their company's borders.

They argue that open innovation is still inherently a linear concept, although technology and ideas can 'move' in and out at all stages.

They argue further that "modern innovation models should once and for all get rid of the notion of linearity in the innovation process" and adopt cyclical concepts of models such as the Cyclic Innovation Model.

In this model, explicit feedback paths are added as well as feed forward options. By harnessing these paths in a cyclical architecture, a dynamic system is created to model an organisation or network and its innovation activities.

This section on innovation has described how innovation has evolved and how more network-friendly cyclical models of innovation offer promise. The use of models such as triple-helix explicitly recognises the value of partnerships and the different stakeholders and their roles in facilitating and supporting innovation.

However, there is one other stakeholder who has occasionally been fully involved in innovation processes around product and service creation and development, but is only now becoming recognised as perhaps the ultimate stakeholder in these processes. That stakeholder is the user, and the following section describes user-driven innovation.

The importance of users in the design process for product and service innovation is increasingly being recognised. It is natural to involve users, and indeed the resulting quality and appropriateness of a product or service suffers in some way if users are not involved in the initial design stages.

What are living labs?

They are collaborations of public-private-civic partnerships in which stakeholders co-create new products, services, businesses and technologies in real life environments.

2.2
USER-DRIVEN INNOVATION

The importance of users in the design process for product and service innovation has long been recognised. It is natural to involve users, and indeed the resulting quality and appropriateness of a product or service suffers in some way if users are not involved in some way in the processes that together make up the design stages.

User-Centred Design (UCD) is an approach that puts the customer or user at the centre of the design process. UCD has been successfully used in many product designs and is supported by standard. The key aim in UCD is to learn what product or service is best suited to meet the needs of the user, and the intended benefit arising from the application of the approach is better usability in the resulting designed product or service.

There is a long tradition of user-orientated, experience-based approaches developed to realise these aims and benefits, including user experience, contextual design, action research and cooperative design.

There are also fresh approaches emerging such as crowdsourcing where design challenges can be opened out to a broad population of people or the wisdom of crowds where it is posited that groups of free-thinking people are likely to make certain types of decisions better than an individual.

But arguably the most interesting is the lead user concept. This concept stems from research finding that it is often the user who can realise a commercially successful product or service, rather than the producers and that a particular type of user, the lead user, may be responsible for the majority of the innovative thinking.

Many of these new approaches in user-centred innovation are facilitated by Information & Communications Technology (ICT), and can thrive in a network economy society. The developers of products and services now have extremely powerful, useful and potentially profitable techniques and approaches that are centred on ICT-supported innovation processes that embrace the customer, citizen or user.

However, while there are models for engagement in innovation partnerships, such as triple-helix, until recently the support has been focused on science parks, business incubators and other activities more related to supporting fledgling new companies, than partnerships that support research and development and innovation activities around new ideas tested with users.

A new paradigm of support has emerged that extends the triple-helix model to involve users, and indeed its name reflects a philosophy of creating a research laboratory where the users are testing products and services; in effect, a living lab.

Some living labs are region-based, others focus on a particular product family, for example, automotive design, while others seek to address particular societal needs in, for example, healthcare or education.

2.3
LIVING LABS

The architect and academic, William J. Mitchell, created the concept of living labs. Mitchell, based at MIT, was interested in how city dwellers could be involved more actively in urban planning and city design.

The idea of citizen involvement in the design process was subsequently taken up and developed further in Europe by various research communities. A small number of living labs, created across Europe in 2005, primarily from the Computer Supported Cooperative Working (CSCW) research community, formed the European Network of Living Labs (ENoLL) in 2006. Successive waves of new living labs have since been created and, in 2010, for example there were 15 living labs in the UK and over 250 living labs across Europe and beyond.

The ENoLL living labs recognise, as did Mitchell, that technology, in particular ICT, plays a powerful catalytic role in user engagement and most living labs are focused on using technology to support user engagement, research novel ways of engaging with users, and communicate findings rapidly and accurately using low-cost, mass-adopted tools such as social networks.

Living labs are "collaborations of public-private-civic partnerships in which stakeholders co-create new products, services, businesses and technologies in real life environments and virtual networks in multi-contextual spheres."

A simpler definition is "a collection of people, equipment, services and technology to provide a test platform for research and experiments." Some position living labs as a kind of technological test-bed while others classify them as "innovation methodologies."

It is apparent from an examination of living labs that many have a particular niche in which they operate. Some labs are region-based, others focus on a particular product family - for example, automotive design - while others seek to address particular societal needs in, for example, healthcare.

However, the use of technology to engage and support users as early as possible in product and service development is the common denominator for all of them.

How living labs actually work centres on methods, processes and services. The methods encompass approaches, tools and techniques that often make use of advanced and innovative applications

of ICT to create and sustain dialogues with users. (For example, analysis of system logs or automatically collected behavioural data, ethnographic research, questionnaires, focus groups, and observation).

The processes are varied but can be described along a development spectrum from the creation of ideas, engagement with user communities and other stakeholders, collection of data using a variety of methods usually facilitated by ICT, and the evaluation of results as well as the methods employed.

These can be summarised as co-creation, exploration, experimentation and evaluation. Another useful perspective on innovation process is the innovation value chain.

PROFILE

TRAIL Living Lab

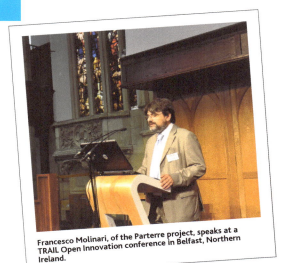

Francesco Molinari, of the Parterre project, speaks at a TRAIL Open Innovation conference in Belfast, Northern Ireland.

Translating Research and Innovation

University of Ulster

The University of Ulster's TRAIL (Translating Research and Innovation Lab) living lab supports research and innovation activities across several key academic disciplines including business, information and communication technologies, occupational therapy, art, health care and media studies.

Based at the University of Ulster, TRAIL is focused on supporting this diverse set of stakeholders as we develop new technologies, research perspectives, processes and integrated service solutions that deliver real value to our users in Northern Ireland, UK and further afield across Europe.

TRAIL adopted the concept of 'living labs', which is a fresh European initiative involving partnerships between public and private entities, with strong involvement of user communities, concentrating on the development of new information services, businesses, technologies and markets, and importantly placing people at the very centre of service and product development and innovation. We established TRAIL as the first living lab in Northern Ireland.

TRAIL is focused on assisting people in the development of user-centred techniques to develop and improve services and products. TRAIL has been particularly interested in assisting ageing, rural dwellers, supporting them in their homes to lead fulfilling lives in the heart of their communities. For example, our Northern Periphery Programme project, called MyHealth@age contributed towards defining health and wellbeing needs of the ageing population on peripheral and remote communities on the northern margins of Europe, specifically Sweden, Norway and Newry, Northern Ireland. Another example of TRAIL engaging with local communities is evidenced

by the PARTERRE project, which is creating participative demographic engagements at grass roots level to tackle key community issues.

TRAIL's vision for engagement with local communities is founded on the evidence that providing grass roots communities and enterprises with tools to engage people in the creative design of solutions to the problems that they face often inspires their thinking and results in outcomes that better match the needs of the community. It's also more fun!

TRAIL works in partnership with many community-orientated enterprises across Northern Ireland and beyond, including, for example: Fold Housing Association, CEDAR Foundation, many of the NHS Health & Social Care Trusts in Northern Ireland, Belfast City Council, Newry City Council and Lisburn City Council.

TRAIL's experience in working with local community-based initiatives supported by UK or European research and innovation funding, is that the engagement is welcomed by the community at all levels. A key value in the engagement is the university building further opportunities for collaboration and development.

trail.ulster.ac.uk

Living labs are "collaborations of public-private-civic partnerships in which stakeholders co-create new products, services, businesses and technologies in real life environments and virtual networks in multi-contextual spheres."

A simpler definition is "a collection of people, equipment, services and technology to provide a test platform for research and experiments." Some position living labs as a kind of technological test-bed while others classify them as "innovation methodologies".

The innovation value chain is viewed as an end-to-end process encompassing three main stages: idea generation, conversion, and diffusion, with conversion including both selection of ideas and their subsequent development.

While the innovation value chain described is generally seen as being controlled by a commercial organisation, the concept can arguably be said to be stronger if the value chain is comprised of a variety of triple-helix stakeholders, each bringing their organisation's strengths to the process.

In addition to these phase processes, other aspects that make living labs different from traditional research and development innovation labs have been described.

These include openness, influence, realism, value and sustainability. The concept of openness is valuable in living labs as it promotes open communication within and without the stakeholder groups in all development phases. However, there are problems in promoting openness while retaining, for example, Intellectual Property (IP) rights.

The principle of realism is a critically important one as it relates to the promotion of concepts where consensus is reached between stakeholders.

Services are a useful way of presenting the stakeholder with a set of 'competencies' with which the living lab is familiar. A living lab can be seen as a "service providing organisation in the topic of Research and Development (R&D) and innovation" with a set of resources including: areas of competency, local partners and stakeholders, ICT infrastructure, operational methodology and administrative resources.

Services in living labs have been listed as co-creation, integration and data preparation. Co-creation is described as a core service facilitating the development of a product, service or application, decomposed further in to four phases, addressing idea, concept, development and market launch of product or service. Integration services centre on making a product or service available to users via the living lab, while data preparation is a harmonised way of preparing and presenting the findings.

Living labs operate within a policy framework in Europe. This framework has evolved, supported by ENoLL and the European Commission, who see a role for living labs, particularly as components in the Competitiveness and Innovation Programme.

There is a broader policy framework in which living labs could be situated, termed Territorial Cohesion. This is defined as "a situation whereby policies to reduce disparities, enhance competitiveness and promote sustainability acquire added value by forming coherent packages, taking account of where they take effect, the specific opportunities and constraints there, now and in the future".

There is an argument for giving living labs a role in a transversal policy where they facilitate a user-centred, open research capability in any engagement or initiative, rather than the current role where living labs are funded much like science parks or incubators using a sectoral policy philosophy.

This "territorial innovation" would be a move away from building specialised research centres, towards integrating research with local and regional development stakeholders and municipalities, involving citizens from all areas of life to address problems affecting the territory.

2.4
CHALLENGES TO USING LIVING LABS

The challenges and issues that are faced by living labs are seen as related to potential problems in each of the areas of infrastructure, methods, tools and policy. Another issue relates to how the research organisations or universities can develop agendas for inter-disciplinary research, which is beneficial to living labs but not to universities that seek to specialise in particular areas of expertise.

> **"There is an argument for giving living labs a role in a transversal policy where they facilitate a user-centred, open research capability in any initiative or engagement."**

Other challenges have been identified as relating to collaboration, standardisation and efficiency. Each living lab has to develop its competencies in user-centred methods and engage with the stakeholders. In terms of standardisation, living labs often carry out very similar practices of engagement but because many living labs have developed from different areas of science, there is no common and agreed vernacular.

Efficiency may be an issue in living labs but the use of ICT to aid communication between stakeholders and users must help to reduce engagement budgets. In general, each of these issues is an issue of living lab standardisation and the presence of a governance organisation means that the living labs should have access to harmonisation and standardisation roadmaps.

The importance of users in the design process for product and service innovation has long been recognised. It is natural to involve users, and indeed the resulting quality and appropriateness of a product or service suffers in some way if users are not involved in some way in the processes that together make up the design stages.

What's important about what you have just read?

• Living labs embody collaboration – living labs offer a collaborative partnership framework in which user-centred, innovation activities can take place.

• Living labs represent a coherent offering – living labs offer methods to garner data and evidence on design. They combine this with processes that develop ideas, oversee engagement with users on how data is evaluated, and then package all the constituent components into a coherent offering that can be understood by the core stakeholder groups i.e. users, businesses, civic partners and research organisations such as universities.

• Living labs have limitations – while they offer unprecedented and structured access to users and their views on products and services, they do not offer such a structured framework for the subsequent exploitation of any improvements and innovations in products and services developed in the labs.

3.0
BEFORE
PARTICIPATION

DEVELOPING A SHARED UNDERSTANDING OF THE PURPOSE OF THE PARTICIPATION EXERCISE IS CRUCIAL - IT HELPS THE PROCESS RUN SMOOTHLY.

In this chapter we will:
• Clarify the purpose of your participation exercise;
• Identify your key stakeholders; and,
• Determine what 'success' looks like in the context of your participation exercise.

3.1 RATIONALE: WHY ARE WE DOING THIS?
User participation exercises take time and resources to execute. The findings from them are intended to influence the future development of a product or service. Therefore, before you embark on any user participation exercise, it is crucial to be clear about your reasons for doing so and what specifically you need to find out.

3.1.1 HOW DO I CLARIFY THE PURPOSE?

Often the best way to clarify the purpose is through team work. A blend of different perspectives acts as healthy challenge and is often more efficient and effective at identifying the real aims than individuals working alone or like individuals working together.

(For more information on the benefits of group working, see the case study in the appendix with references to 'group think').

One way to do this is to bring together representatives from the community, the business sector and academia – for a dedicated workshop, or facilitated meeting, to work on developing a shared understanding of the purpose of the participation exercise.

Another way is to create partnerships among all key stakeholder groups and invite them to sit in your Steering Committee as they can advise you on many aspects of user involvement.

The importance of this cannot be overstated. Developing a shared understanding from the outset is highly beneficial in two important ways:

• It helps set everyone's expectations i.e. all parties know what they are 'getting into'; and,

• It helps secure commitment from all involved and helps the participation exercise run more smoothly. People who have actively contributed to the design of a process are more likely to support it.

A participation exercise can have more than one purpose and you will need to be very clear what yours is/are if you want to get the most from it. Whatever your purpose(s), you are always, at some level, looking for information on knowledge, attitudes and/or behaviours.

One of the most helpful ways to express the purpose of your participation exercise is as a series of written questions. For example, you could say, "In our participation exercise, we want to find out..."

• What do users know about a specific product / service? (knowledge)

• What are their views on it? (attitudes)
• Do they use it, not use it? (Behaviour) and why (Attitudes)

• How do users think this product or service could be better? (Knowledge, Attitudes)."

If your list of questions becomes unwieldy it is less easy to manage, therefore, keep your list as concise and precise as possible.

3.1.2 HOW WILL I KNOW WHEN I HAVE CLARIFIED THE PURPOSE OF THE PARTICIPATION EXERCISE?

The easiest way to do this is to ask yourself and your team, 'If we had the answers to these questions, what would or could we do with them?'

If you can answer that easily, you have clarified the purpose of your participation exercise. If you cannot do this easily, you probably need to refine your questions and make them more specific until it is clear that the answers will be of value and can be used readily. This could mean specifying particular groups of users that are of special interest to you (e.g. gender, age bands, disability, martial status, people with dependents, people in urban / rural areas, people from different social classes etc) and focusing the participation exercise specifically on them.

For example, rather than say,
"In our participation exercise, we want to find out what users know about a specific product / service?"
We might refine this to say:
"In our participation exercise, we want to find out what do women aged 70 or over, who have had a hip operation in the last 12 months, and who live in a rural area, know about a specific product / service?"

3.1.3
PERHAPS THE ANSWERS TO THESE QUESTIONS ARE ALREADY KNOWN? DO WE REALLY NEED A PARTICIPATION EXERCISE?

This is a critical question in itself since carrying out a participation exercise typically takes a considerable amount of time and resources. It is therefore only to be embarked on when it is clear that the answers to the questions above can only be obtained by carrying out a participation exercise. For example, on occasions, some or all of the answers to the questions posed could be found by other means e.g. literature reviews, examining existing databases etc.

Consequently, it is good practice to trawl existing literature and data first. Often such a search provides partial answers/ insights to the questions posed and the initial set of questions is consequently revised.

Ultimately, you and your team have to discern:
a. which questions cannot be answered by a search of the literature and existing databases; and consequently,
b. which questions merit a participation exercise.

3.1.4
ONCE I HAVE CLARIFIED THE PURPOSE OF THE PARTICIPATION EXERCISE, THEN WHAT DO I DO?

Once these have been agreed on, it is important to document them and share them with all those who contributed to them so that all parties involved have a written record of the scope of the exercise. This is called the 'terms of reference' for the participation exercise. This is a crucial document which will be referenced frequently as the participation exercise proceeds. Time invested now clarifying the purpose, will pay dividends later down the line.

3.2
WHO NEEDS TO PARTICIPATE?

3.2.1
IDENTIFYING STAKEHOLDERS

One of your first tasks will be figuring out who you will need to consult. Again team work is most effective for this.

Ask your team, what 'type' of users do we need to consult? What are their characteristics e.g. gender, age, location, social class, disability etc?

Also, within any broad group of users (e.g. users with a learning disability), what specific characteristics are of interest? For example, you may wish to seek the views of:

- adults (people aged 18 and over) with a mild to moderate learning disability; or
- adults with a profound learning disability; or,
- adults with a mild to moderate learning disability who also have a sensory impairment.

Be specific about the characteristics of the user groups you need to involve.

Beyond users themselves, think also about who else you need to involve. For example, in the above case, you may wish to design a participation exercise that takes into account the experiences and views of carers, key workers, key influencers (e.g. relevant community or voluntary groups, network organizations) and/or key decision makers or who make policy or fund services for people with learning disability.

When you think about who else to involve, think broadly because in essence you are trying to capture as diverse a range of views as possible within the budget and time allowance you have. Typically, the broader the range of views, the richer and more robust the insight will be.

3.2.2
MAPPING STAKEHOLDERS

A 'stakeholder' is someone who can potentially add insight to your participation exercise. This someone could be an individual or a group or organisation.

When we talk about 'mapping stakeholders' we are simply referring to a process whereby, using simple notation, we can represent our understanding of:

• who the key stakeholders are; and,
• our relationship with them.

There are many different ways to 'map' stakeholders. The notation below is only one way. For example, let's imagine the local police force wanted to carry out a participation exercise to engage local people, local businesses and local academics to work out what would help reduce crime in the local town centre. The stakeholder map corresponding to this might look something like that illustrated.

In this imaginary setting, the local police have strong positive relationships with the statutory bodies, local partnerships, community and voluntary groups, clubs and societies but weaker relationships with schools, churches and local businesses.

It is also clear from this example, that any participation exercise involving organised criminals, offenders and victims of crime is likely to prove problematic given the barriers inherent in engaging with these groupings. Finally, whilst there do not appear to be any major barriers to engaging with academics or the media, the diagram makes it clear that relationships between these bodies and the local police need to be strengthened.

KEY

Name of Stakeholder
Strong/positive relationship exists
Weak relationship exists
Weak relationship plus a FEW known barriers to involvement
Weak relationship plus MULTIPLE known barriers to involvement

Stakeholder Map

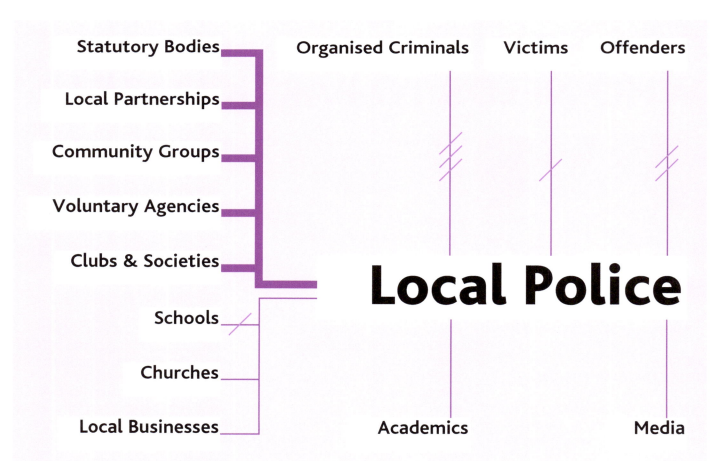

A stakeholder is someone who can potentially add insight to your participation exercise.

This someone could be an individual or a group or organization. When we talk about 'mapping stakeholders' we are simply referring to a process whereby, using simple notation, we can represent our understanding of who the key stakeholders are and our relationship with them.

3.2.3 PRIORITISING STAKEHOLDERS

In any participation exercise, the views of some stakeholders are going to be more significant than others. Before embarking on your participation exercise, it is important to understand which stakeholders' views are the most significant for your particular study because this has direct implications for the amount of effort you are going to expend involving them i.e. seeking their views, analysing the feedback they give you and feeding back to them.

The figure below is called a **'Power/Interest' Matrix.**

'**POWER**' is a measure of the amount of authority or influence a particular stakeholder has/can have over the future development of your product/ service. This 'power' could be in at least two forms.

• '**Bureaucratic**' power i.e. The stakeholder holds a designated position of authority over e.g. legal matters, policies or funds; or

• '**Collective power**' – Whilst the views of an individual citizen or group may not make much difference to the plans for your product or service, when if individuals or groups (e.g. Trade Unions, network organizations) act together, the level of 'collective power' they may acquire could be considerable. Consequently, it is important to acknowledge the following.

'**INTEREST**' is a measure of how much attention the stakeholder either typically gives or is likely to give to your product service and developments thereof.

For example, it cannot be automatically assumed that simply because a stakeholder has high level of bureaucratic power in a particular area that they will automatically have a high level of interest in that area.

Powerful stakeholders typically have multiple responsibilities and, depending on the pressures prevailing at any moment in time, they may be required to focus their attention (interest) on an area not linked with your product or service. Hence, they could have a high level of 'power' but low interest.

Conversely, simply because an individual has an intense interest in your subject does not automatically mean that they are in a prime position to influence key issues related to it.

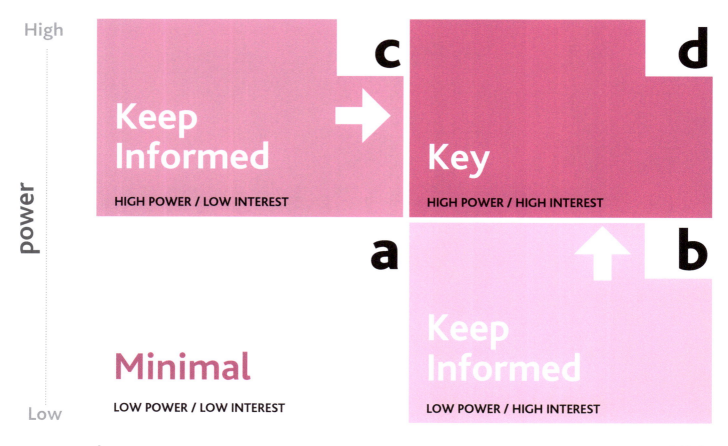

Power/Interest Matrix

To prioritise stakeholders, simply take the list of stakeholders you identified in the mapping exercise and place each of them in one of the above four quadrants of the Power/Interest matrix. Each stakeholder will be placed in one of the following four quadrants:

c

HIGH POWER/LOW INTEREST

These stakeholders may be either temporarily less interested in your product / service (e.g. due to workload or other more pressing responsibilities). In which case, it would be helpful to invest some resources in keeping them informed. If the context changes, and they become interested, their influence could be highly significant. Some stakeholders in this category may have power but may never acquire an interest in your product/ service. Keeping such stakeholders informed becomes more a matter of professional courtesy but nonetheless is helpful if done.

d

HIGH POWER/HIGH INTEREST

These stakeholders are the key players. Invest the greatest proportion of your resources in actively involving these players, building relationships with them, analysing their feedback closely, and taking special note of key positive and negative points that emerge.

a

LOW POWER/LOW INTEREST

You will invest only minimal effort in involving these stakeholders. Their views will have very little influence on the future direction of your product / service.

b

LOW POWER/HIGH INTEREST

These stakeholders are very interested in what you are doing but have little real influence over your product or service. Invest some effort keeping these stakeholders informed. Being enthusiastic about your product or service, they can be good allies generally. It also possible for stakeholders in this group to 'move' into Quadrant D, where they could potentially influence matters hugely. Building the relationships now is an investment.

3.3 WHAT DOES SUCCESS LOOK LIKE? In other words, how can we tell how effective the participation exercise has been? For this to be evaluated effectively, we need some way to measure our performance, which in itself, needs very careful consideration.

"No single measure is likely to tell the full story and so, it is important that you select a range of measures, to assess the 'success' of the participation exercise. Assess and select the best practise principles which are most important to your key players, those with the greatest level of power and interest."

A key issue when preparing for participation is trying to determine, 'What will 'success' look like?'. In other words, how can we tell how effective the participation exercise has been?

We need some way to measure our 'performance'. However, in practice, this needs careful consideration because typically what constitutes 'success', in a participation exercise, will differ for each segment of stakeholder i.e. academic, business, community and user.

For example, users will typically perceive 'success' as their suggestions etc. being taken on board, whilst academic and business stakeholders will have quite different parameters that define 'success' for them.

The key is to ensure that you are clear on, and take account of, what defines 'success' for your most powerful and interested stakeholders – whether they be users, academic, business or community – and that you build into your participation exercise, ways of capturing information that helps you assess 'success' as you go along. The sheer diversity of participation exercises, combined with the diverse perceptions of 'success' across the stakeholder segments themselves, means that any attempt at defining 'success' needs to be sufficiently flexible to encompass these elements.

All participation exercises are based on fundamental principles (See Section 1.5) and adherence to these principles is important when determining how to measure the 'success' of your participation exercise.

No single measure is likely to tell the full story and so, it is important that you select a range of measures, to assess the 'success' of the participation exercise. The best way to select a) these measures of success, and b) the processes to gather the necessary evidence, is a group exercise or workshop involving key representatives from the relevant parties.

The outcome you are seeking from this is a shared understanding and consensus amongst the key players on a) the choice of 'success' measures and b) the processes that will be used to gather the data necessary to assess 'success'.

For example, if your participation was trying to find ways to reduce social isolation for older people in your local town and rural hinterlands during winter months, your workshop might (say taking the Principle of 'Inclusion' as an example) identify a range of measures to assess effectiveness relating to this, including those shown on the following page.

Success Assessment

Type of measure	Description of the Measure	Process to Gather the Data
INPUT	Total number and profile of older people consulted	Count and analyse the numbers and types of older people who took part.
OUTPUT	Clear identification and prioritisation of key issues that older people say would reduce social isolation for them.	Listen to the experiences and views of older people, their advocates, key service providers, policy makers and academics who have studied these challenges.
OUTCOME	Specific changes to service provision that impact directly on the issues identified above, particularly the priority issues.	Record views, intentions and decisions of key policy makers and service providers following their consideration of the findings from the participation exercise. Note what will change.

3.4 WHAT SHAPE SHOULD MY PARTICIPATION EXERCISE TAKE?

By now, you have determined:
• What you want to find out;
• Who needs to participate;
• The key players whom you need to involve; and,
• How you are going to measure 'success'.
Now you are ready to explore how you are going to do this i.e. what method(s) you are going to use.

What's important about what you have just read?

Measuring Success

Be clear on the purpose of the participation exercise – Make sure that there is a shared understanding of this across your stakeholders. These debates in themselves yield useful insights which are hugely beneficial to any participation exercise. Invest the majority of your time and resources into involving the 'Key Players' i.e. those stakeholders with the greatest level of Power and Interest.

Again, look at the best practice principles and ask yourself, 'Which of these is most important to the 'Key Players', make sure you have defined appropriate indicators of success that relate to these principles and that you have a strong evidence cluster i.e., evidence of 'success' being collected via different methods from different parts of the participation exercise.

Do the prioritising of stakeholders with others. There are usually different views on who really holds 'power' or is 'interested'.

4.0
DURING PARTICIPATION

FAVOUR METHODS THAT BEST SUIT THE 'KEY PLAYERS'; THOSE PEOPLE WHOSE VIEWS ARE MOST IMPORTANT IN HELPING YOU GAIN THE INSIGHT THAT YOU NEED

This chapter is about the various methods you can use in user participation exercises. To do this, we will look at:

- The two main types of user participation – quantitative and qualitative;
- Key points that you need to consider irrespective of which type you propose to use;
- A range of quantitative and qualitative methods that are commonly used and how you can deploy these in your participation exercises;
- Mixed methods - Approaches that use a combination of quantitative and qualitative methods;
- Emerging methods – Methods that use internet-based information technology; and,
- The strengths and weaknesses of the above methods in the context of participation exercises.

4.1 TYPES OF USER PARTICIPATION

There are two types of research methods that involve users. These are Quantitative methods, which generate statistical information, and Qualitative methods, which broadly explore attitudes and behaviour.

4.1.1 WHAT ARE THE TWO MAIN TYPES?

There are basically two types of research involving users:

QUANTITATIVE
which generates statistical information;

QUALITATIVE
which explores attitudes, experience and behaviour.

QUANTITATIVE RESEARCH
The main methods in quantitative research are surveys or questionnaires.

If you have ever been stopped on the street by a researcher or if you have filled in a questionnaire that came through the post, this would be classed as quantitative research.

This type of research reaches many more participants, but the actual contact time with each participant is much shorter than it is in qualitative research.

QUALITATIVE RESEARCH
The methods used in qualitative research include interviews or group discussions (e.g. focus groups).

This type of research tries to get an in-depth opinion from participants. The questions the participants are asked relate to attitudes, behaviour and experiences.

These concepts are multi-faceted and often inter-related. Hence, there is a degree of exploring and clarifying within the process itself.

This takes time and consequently, the contact time per individual participant tends to be a lot longer compared with quantitative research.

The additional time required per participant means that, in practice, qualitative research processes can usually only be afforded with a relatively small number of participants in any one participation exercise.

In addition, there is, what we will refer to as, mixed methods, i.e. methods that combine elements of quantitative and qualitative research approaches when engaging participants.

4.1.2 IS ONE TYPE BETTER THAN THE OTHER? The short answer is that no one method is intrinsically better than another. For example, there is a common misconception that quantitative research is somehow 'better' than qualitative research, perceived as more 'scientific' – simply by virtue of its being numerically based.

The reality, however, is neither method is better than the other — they are simply different and both have their strengths and weaknesses. Indeed, the relative strengths and weaknesses of the various approaches should be understood, considered and acknowledged by those designing, conducting and reporting on the participation exercise.

Moreover, the suitability and value of a particular method and the quality of insight that can be gleaned from it will depend on a range of factors, not just the method itself, but how it is used and, importantly, how it is subsequently analysed.

In many cases, a combination of quantitative and qualitative methods provides the best potential for gathering insights into participants' opinions, experiences and behaviours in relation to a specific initiative. In research, this type of comparison is called 'triangulation'.

For example, one of the ways to test the reliability of your findings is to compare the key themes emerging from one source using one method (e.g. a survey with a specific segment of participants) with the themes that emerge when you use the same source but a different method (e.g. a series of focus groups with the same segment of participants).

Consistency in the themes emerging can be a useful finding (i.e. as possible evidence, in this case, to support your interpretation of the survey results). Equally, it can be thought provoking — and potentially even advantageous - if the messages from the focus group work give you reason to question your original interpretation of the survey results.

This might suggest that a deeper and / or wider understanding of the issues needs to be obtained before any definitive conclusions can be drawn.

4.1.3
DECIDING WHICH APPROACH IS RIGHT FOR YOU

Your choice of methods will be influenced, to some extent, by what method or combination of methods is likely to yield the greatest level of insight at the lowest cost, in the shortest timescale, and with the least burden on the participants. In addition, be aware that your stakeholders, and your key players in particular, might prefer one approach over the other. If this is the case, consider carefully if their preferences can be met alongside other considerations e.g. cost, available resources and skills and experience.

4.2 KEY POINTS YOU NEED TO CONSIDER

Irrespective of the type of method you use, there are a number of general points you need to consider, including:

SAMPLE
How to identify who needs to take part.

MAXIMISING PARTICIPATION
How to maximise the level and quality of participation.

ANALYSIS
How to analyse the data you have collected.

RELIABILITY
How to maximise the reliability and accuracy of the findings.

SKILLS / EQUIPMENT
How to ascertain what skills and/or equipment will be required to a) gather the data and b) analyse the findings. There will always be decisions to be made about what it would be desirable to do in terms of participation and what can actually be afforded in terms of the time and money available.

Hence, you will also need to consider:

TIMESCALE
How long will a particular method take to implement?

MONEY
What is it likely to cost?

A further general point you will need to consider alongside all of the above is:

PILOTING
How you intend to try out a specific method and/or an aspect of a method on a small number of participants, and learning what 'works' and does not 'work, and refining your approach, before extending the revised process to a larger number.

For example, you might try out a draft questionnaire, or a discussion guide for a focus group on a small number of participants and assess, for example, how clearly (or not) the questions are understood, how are participants interacting with the questions.

You could also, or instead, use a pilot to test a specific aspect of a proposed participation approach. For example, you might wish to assess how much (or little) participants demonstrate a willingness to engage when offered a particular type or level of incentive, or when it is proposed that the discussions take place at different venues (e.g. somewhere close by participants compared with somewhere further away).

Investments in the pilot phase typically yield crucial insights and often save considerable time and money in the long run. The basic point is, if time and money are major factors for your participation exercise, running pilots becomes more, not less, important! All of these points are covered in detail in this chapter.

In relation to any particular method, you will need to know what the method actually involves and how data is collected. In order to make an informed choice on the most appropriate method, you will also need to understand, not just the process but the main advantages and disadvantages of that particular method as well. Again, this is covered in detail in this chapter.

PROFILE

The PEOPPLE Project

Putting Evidence for Older People into Practice in Living Environments

School of Health Sciences and Social Work,
University of Portsmouth

This project, funded by the UK Higher Education Innovation Fund, aims to address some of the unmet needs of older people living in the local community in the Portsmouth area.

Central to this study is a desire to establish and maintain strong links with local older people and to maximise user involvement. We use the term 'user involvement' as defined by INVOLVE (www.invo.org.uk): An active partnership between the public and researchers in the research process, rather than the use of people as the 'subjects' of research.

To help achieve this is it was agreed that the University would work in partnership with key organisations who would be central to engaging with the local community and collaborators on the study. In addition, members of the public are part of the project team and Steering Group.

Identifying the Themes:
The first phase of the project aimed to ascertain important issues relevant to the local older person's community. This was achieved through a series of workshops, focus groups and interviews. Older people were engaged through local groups, clubs, and organisations, articles in newsletters and posters in community centres.

Members of the public and local group leaders advised on appropriate materials, logo, ways of conducting the involvement, and ethical aspects of the project. Information was posted on a webpage specifically designed for the project (www.port.ac.uk/peopple).

A sample grid was designed to ensure inclusion of people from different backgrounds and areas. Materials were translated in Chinese and Bangladeshi (these are the biggest local ethnic minority communities), and produced in enlarged format and CDs for people with visual difficulties. Free transportation, refreshments and snacks were offered to all. A 'thank you' gift voucher was given to each person at the end of their involvement.

Generating the questions and seeking the evidence:
In the second phase of the work, two community workshops involving local older people were held to generate a set of focused and prioritised questions based on the themes generated in the first phase. The third phase of the project involves a synthesis of the evidence base as governed by the questions identified earlier. In this phase lay members help assess the evidence. This phase identifies appropriate means of addressing the selected issues as well as identifying gaps in the evidence which require new innovations.

Presenting the evidence and implementation projects:
The findings are fed back to the community to assess how receptive people are to the proposed solutions, and how these may be tailored to individual needs, circumstances, and beliefs.

This work involves the evaluation of interventions to help target the needs of older people. Interventions may be products, devices, or services geared towards improving wellbeing and quality of life. It is anticipated that the local community will continue to be actively involved in the planning, delivery, evaluation and dissemination of the work.

Researchers from the School of Health Sciences and Social Work at the University of Portsmouth host a meeting as part of the PEOPPLE project.

www.port.ac.uk/peopple

4.3 QUANTITIVE METHODS
4.3.1 WHAT'S THAT?
Summarised information using numbers or statistics.

"When designing any survey one of the most important considerations is how to make sure that the respondents who take part in the survey are representative of the group of interest or those we are interested in targeting."

By quantitative methods we are referring to information which is summarised using numbers or statistics.

Within a research sense this information can relate to people's knowledge, attitudes and behaviour and is used to describe how particular groups within society interact with the world around them.

When referring to quantitative methods we usually refer to surveys which are carried out to address an information gap or the use of information which has already been collected by government or other organisations within society.

Using existing quantitative information is normally referred to as 'secondary data analysis' and is always a useful starting point when planning any research project involving the collection of new information by using a survey.

By reviewing existing information it will be easier to prioritise what new information is needed through a survey.

This review will also help in shaping the content and structure of the survey questionnaire in line with the information needs of your participation exercise.

4.3.2
HOW DO I PLAN A SURVEY?

When planning a survey there are a number of important things to consider such as:

How to identify and draw a sample of respondents?

How many people need to take part?

How will the information be collected?

How to get a good response rate?

Can the reliability and accuracy of the findings be guaranteed?

What will it cost?

How long will it take?

How will the collected information be processed?

What skills will be required to analyse the findings?

What other skills or assistance will be required?

4.3.3
SAMPLING: WHAT ARE THE MAIN POINTS TO CONSIDER? SELECTING RESPONDENTS OR SAMPLING

When designing any survey one of the most important considerations is how to make sure that the respondents who take part in the survey are representative of those we are interested in targeting (i.e. the target population).

If the survey respondents are not representative of the group from which they are drawn then survey bias becomes a problem. This is when particular groups (e.g. men or women and people of particular age groups etc) may be either underrepresented or over represented in the sample. Generally two types of sampling methods which can be used to help avoid survey bias: random sampling; and, quota sampling.

WHAT IS RANDOM SAMPLING?

Random sampling as its name suggests means that everyone in the group or population of interest has an equal chance of being selected to take part in the survey (a bit like taking balls out of a hat!). Depending on which method of collecting data is being used, pure random sampling can be quite expensive, particularly if using face-to-face interviewing and respondents are very dispersed.

There are different types of random sampling methods however the most common is stratified random sampling which allows the sample to be designed to take account of what is already known about a population or group of interest.

Required sample sizes depending on population homogeneity and desired accuracy

Acceptable Sampling Error (+/-)	% of population likely to give a particular answer (95% Confidence Level)					
	5 or 95	10 or 90	20 or 80	30 or 70	40 or 60	50 / 50
1	1900	3600	6400	8400	9600	10,000
2	479	900	1600	2100	2400	2500
3	211	400	711	933	1066	1100
4	119	225	400	525	600	625
5	76	144	256	336	370	400
6	a	100	178	233	267	277
7	-	73	131	171	192	204
8	-	-	100	131	150	156
9	-	-	79	104	117	123
10	-	-	-	84	96	100

(a) Samples smaller than this would normally be too small to allow meaningful analysis.

For example, if we are surveying a local community and we know the proportion of people living in different administrative areas within the community then we can make sure that this breakdown is reflected in the sample.

Similarly, if we know that users of a particular service are 80% women, then we can ensure that our sample is made up of 80% women and 20% men.

WHAT IS QUOTA SAMPLING?

Quota sampling or convenience sampling is an alternative to random sampling where the selection of the sample is made by the interviewer who has been given quotas to fill from specified subgroups of the population.

For example, an interviewer may be told to interview 100 females aged between 30 and 49. Quota sample is usually quick and cheap to carry out. However, because it is non-random it is impossible to

say what the sampling error is (i.e. how precise the information is).

HOW DO I DETERMINE A SAMPLE SIZE?

As a general rule, the larger the sample the better it is at estimating things about the population. When deciding on a sample size a number of considerations come into play including: how accurate and reliable does the information need to be or what level of error is acceptable; the cost of conducting fieldwork; and, whether or not we need to examine differences between subgroups within the sample (e.g. within a user survey we may need to examine differences between high volume users and low volume users).

WHAT IS SAMPLING ERROR?

There is a close relationship between sample size and what we call sampling error which gives us some idea of how precise our survey estimates are. The table above sets out this relationship between

sample size and sample error and shows that the greater the sample size is the more precise the estimates are.

As an example, if we are carrying out a survey of 1100 users then we know that if 50% of users are satisfied with the service or product being supplied, then we can be 95% confident that the true level of satisfaction among all users lies somewhere between 47% and 53% (i.e. the sampling error is + / 3% based on a sample size of 1100).

Likewise, if we have surveyed 100 users then we can be 95% confident that the true level of satisfaction with the product or service lies somewhere between 40% and 60% (i.e. the sampling error is + / - 10% based on a sample size of 100).

Note that these examples have been presented at the 95% level, but it is possible to apply greater levels of precision such as the 99% level and the 99.9% level.

SAMPLE LISTS AND SOURCES

For most surveys researchers use lists of households, individuals or organisations from which samples are drawn.

Commercial companies such as postal and marketing companies can supply lists of households and individuals at a cost.

These lists are normally supplied in electronic format and will hold the key contact information needed to access respondents.

A first step is to make sure the sample list is comprehensive and includes all members of the population or target group of interest.

Some individuals and households will have opted to have their details removed from such lists s oalways try to establish some sense of how complete or comprehensive the list is.

Lists can be broken down by different groups or areas which may help in designing a sample, making it easier to make selections on the basis of characteristics of interest such as social class, socio-economic status or the level of deprivation within an area.

Many lists of households and individuals have telephone numbers, addresses and other useful information appended.

Some lists will be updated on a more regular basis than others. All lists will have incorrect or obsolete information which may impact on aspects of survey fieldwork.

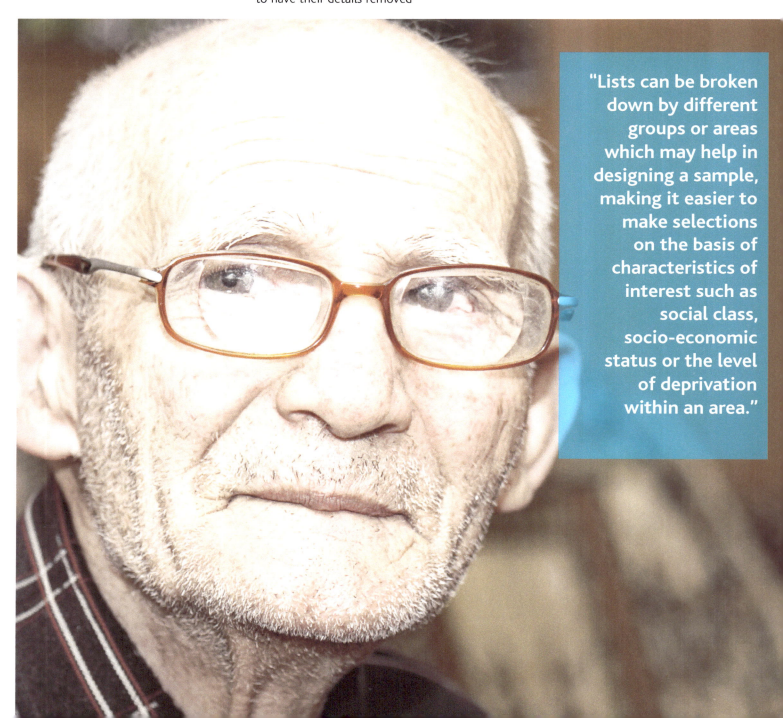

"Lists can be broken down by different groups or areas which may help in designing a sample, making it easier to make selections on the basis of characteristics of interest such as social class, socio-economic status or the level of deprivation within an area."

4.3.4
WHAT ARE THE MAIN DATA COLLECTION METHODS?

With any survey, information can be collected using one of two ways: **1.** Interviewer administered, where an interviewer asks a respondent questions; **2.** Self-completion, where the respondent completes the survey on their own.
Within each of these there are different techniques one could use to gather the data.

INTERVIEWER ADMINISTERED SURVEYS: STRENGTHS AND WEAKNESSES

There are a number of advantages with interviewer administered surveys such as better quality information because the interviewer can assist and interact with the respondent to ensure that no questions are misunderstood and that all questions are completed.

Interviewer administered surveys will normally generate a higher response rate and also offer the opportunity to find out about respondents who refused to take part or could not take part due to other reasons such as illness. Information on non-response is very helpful in assessing the representativeness of the survey.

There are also a number of limitations with interviewer administered surveys, the increased cost being primary among these.

Other limitations include: respondents not wanting to give private or sensitive information to a stranger; bias can creep in with respondents wanting to either impress the interviewer, or provide the interviewer with socially desirable responses; and, interviewer administered surveys can take longer to carry out.

DIFFERENT TYPES OF INTERVIEWER ADMINISTERED SURVEY

With interviewer administered surveys, the survey can be conducted using traditional pen and paper or by using computer technology (i.e. Computer Assisted Personal Interviewing, or CAPI, normally using a laptop computer or handheld Personal Digital Assistant or PDA). Regardless of which method is used there are standard procedures which should be applied to ensure that the survey is successful, namely: use experienced interviewers; brief interviewers in advance; put in place quality control procedures such as checking with respondents on how the survey was carried out.

If using CAPI the survey will benefit because of the facility of pre-programming the questionnaire. This will mean that skips and logic filters between questions will automatically route respondents through the questionnaire. This will improve the quality of the data collected by ensuring that questions can only be answered a particular way and that responses must be logically correct. This will also reduce the amount of time required to clean or validate the survey data file before analysis.

Using CAPI also means that it is possible to play sound and video clips within the interview as well as being able to record verbatim respondents' answers to particular questions. This can be important when carrying out research to determine awareness of, or exposure to, campaigns on radio, television or the printed press. CAPI devices are also highly portable with some slightly larger than a smart phone.

Telephone interviewing is another option for interviewer administered surveys. With telephone interviewing a paper copy questionnaire can be used or alternatively the questionnaire can be pre programmed as a CATI or Computer Assisted Telephone Interview.

Telephone interviews can produce high response rates but their success is dependent on having an up to date sample of telephone numbers for respondents. Getting a reliable sample for households for example can be difficult with many householders opting to have their telephone number removed from marketing lists. It is good practice to first of all establish how reliable and complete the sample of telephone numbers is. Many companies can supply lists of telephone numbers for this purpose but always check the quality of the list by enquiring about the source for the list as well as how often it is updated.

> **"There are also a number of limitations with interviewer administered surveys, the increased cost being primary among these."**

Traditionally most households would have had a landline telephone number but with greater reliance on mobile phones carrying out household surveys by telephone has become more difficult as comprehensive lists of mobile telephone numbers are more difficult to access. Also many people will regularly change their mobile number which means that existing lists can become outdated quite quickly.

> **'It is also important to be aware of the significant limitations associated with self-completion surveys, with the chief concern being low response rates. In some community or population surveys the response rate from self-completion surveys can be as low as 5%."**

However, if for example a user survey is being carried out and the sampling frame of telephone numbers is reasonably complete, then telephone interviewing is a viable and cost effective option, particularly if those on the list or sampling frame have given their consent for them to be contacted. If this is the case it is good practice to send an advance letter to respondents advising them of the survey and it is likely that they will be contacted to participate in the survey. This should be mailed 2 to 3 days prior to interview.

When conducting telephone surveys it is vitally important to develop a script for interviewers to follow. The objective with any interviewer administered survey is to ensure that the interview is delivered the same way for each respondent. This ensures consistency in the responses. With this in mind it is always good practice to brief interviewers on the use of the script as well as getting them to conduct test interviews. It is also important that interviewers are briefed on the aim of the survey and be able to answer any straightforward queries from respondents.

The time of day when telephone surveys are conducted is vitally important with surveys of the population best conducted in the evenings (6pm to 9pm) and at weekends when people are likely to be at home and available. For business or user surveys, time of day is not a major factor with anytime during business hours normally appropriate.

If contacting a respondent for interview and they are unable to take part in the survey there and then, offer them the option of taking part later or provide them with a telephone number to allow them to call and take part in the survey at a time convenient to them. Always be flexible and make it as easy as possible for respondents take part in the survey.

Other points to remember about telephone surveys include: be honest with respondents and tell them how long it will take; always explain the rationale for the survey and that it is voluntary; try and make the survey interesting and enjoyable; reassure respondents about anonymity and confidentiality; and, always thank them for their participation.

SELF-COMPLETION SURVEYS STRENGTHS AND WEAKNESSES

The main attraction of using self-completion surveys is the relatively lower cost compared with using interviewers. Self-completion surveys also allow for the coverage of a larger geographical spread and to cross national and international boundaries, particularly with the growth of internet and other digital technologies. These surveys also benefit from being free of interviewer bias and can be useful in cases where the survey topic is sensitive, with respondents able to complete the survey in private.

It is also important to be aware of the significant limitations associated with self-completion surveys, with the chief concern being low response rates. In some community or population surveys the response rate from self-completion surveys can be as low as 5% which seriously undermines the representativeness of the achieved sample. Furthermore, respondents may not complete all of the questions or indeed may not understand some or all of the questions.

DIFFERENT TYPES OF SELF-COMPLETION SURVEY

Postal surveys can be an effective and low cost way of collecting data, with no travelling expenses, interviewer bias, or restrictions on geography. However, the key weakness with this method is the relatively low response rate compared with other methods. They also require the questionnaire to be relatively short and there is always the risk of questions

being misinterpreted.
Nevertheless surveying by post is a popular data collection method.
To ensure the best level of success with postal surveys there are a number of guidelines to follow.

First of all, postal surveys should be accompanied by a covering letter which sets out why the survey is being conducted; that respondent's views are extremely important and their response is valued; how long the survey will take to complete; instructions for completing and returning the survey questionnaire; reassurance regarding anonymity and confidentiality; a closing date; and the contact details for those conducting the survey, should respondents have any queries.

Taking parting in a postal survey should be at zero cost to respondents, with a freepost return envelope included with the covering letter and questionnaire. After the initial mailing it is good practice to send a reminder/thank you letter on the two week anniversary of the mail out. Subsequent reminders are not particularly effective.

As already mentioned a low response rate can be a problem with postal surveys. To counteract this some organisations will increase the size of the sample to make sure a sufficient number of respondents take part. For example, if we need 2000 completed questionnaires and we know the response rate is likely to be around 20%, there is the option of increasing the initial sample to 10,000. This will generate an achieved sample of 2000 cases but we are still faced with the problem of representativeness.

To ensure representativeness it may be possible to correct for the over or under-representation of particular groups. This is called weighting and is a statistical procedure which is applied to the survey data file when the characteristics of the population are known. Weighting can be applied to any survey to correct for bias in respondent profile.

Online surveys are becoming increasingly popular not least because they are relatively low cost to setup and administer. However, the problems with self-completion surveys apply as much to online surveys as postal and other methods with low response rates and representativeness the main problems. Online surveys can be effective within specific contexts where the respondent has an association or affinity with the organisation conducting the research, with employee and customer research examples of where this method has found to be effective.

Online surveys can be passive or active with an example of a passive online survey being a feedback link or form listed on a website. The more active forms however use pop ups to invite website visitors to give their views on a particular topic. The downside with pop ups is that quite often potential respondents see these as irritating and intrusive. Potential respondents can also be sent a web link inviting their participation in the survey with the web link listed in a covering email to respondents. Respondents simply click on the web link and are taken directly to the survey questionnaire.

Reminder emails can be triggered at regular intervals to encourage a higher response rate. If a customer or user survey is being conducted online, there is also the option of using staff with the organisation to promote the survey and to help encourage and direct respondents to the survey.

4.3.5 HOW DO I MAXIMISE RESPONSE RATES? A key challenge with any survey is to try and maximise the response rate. With a higher response rate, the risk of ending up with data that is different from the population from which the survey is drawn, is minimised.

If a reliable sampling method has been used (e.g. random sampling), and a good response rate is achieved, then there will be more confidence in the survey results. There are a number of things you can do to help improve survey response rates:

SEND AN ADVANCE LETTER

Where possible send an advance letter to potential respondents introducing the survey and why it is being carried out. This advanced letter should set out when the survey is to be conducted, and when an interviewer is likely to call. The following points should also be highlighted in the letter:

the anonymity and confidentiality of responses; what is required of the respondent; why and how they were selected; how long the survey will take to complete; contact details should they wish to make contact; and, the value of respondent opinion.

To enhance the credibility of the survey, use the official headed paper of the sponsoring organisation rather than that of a market research company.

Response rates can also be improved if the survey can be done in collaboration with a charitable organisation or other not-for-profit organisation with a high level of social brand awareness.

For example it may be possible to get a not-for-profit organisation to support the charity with an accompanying letter, which mentions that the charity will benefit by a monetary amount for everyone who takes part.

HARNESS THE LOCAL MEDIA

Building partnerships with local media can also help build a positive profile for a survey within local communities. This approach can help promote awareness of the survey and help underscore the importance of people's views in shaping change. Use of the media can also improve access to respondents for interviewers.

ENSURE THE INTERVIEWER IS CLEAR ON THEIR ROLE

Ensure that all interviewers are briefed in advance of fieldwork. The aim of this briefing should be to ensure interviewers have a good understanding of how respondents are to be selected; improve interviewees understanding of the questionnaire; and help instill a good understanding of the why the survey is being conducted to allow them to address any points raised by respondents.

Interviewer briefings should also focus on timescale, quality assurance procedures and procedures for returning completed interviews either in paper copy or electronically if Computer Assisted Personal Interviewing is used. Finally, interviewers should also be briefed to always carry their identification card.

ENSURE THAT SUFFICIENT AND APPROPRIATE ATTEMPTS ARE MADE TO SECURE A RESPONSE

If a survey is being conducted using random sampling at pre-selected addresses, it is important that more than one attempt is made by interviewers to try and secure an interview at that address.

In most surveys of this type, interviewers are instructed to make up to 3 call backs to try and get an interview with the person or household listed in the sampling frame.

This can be quite costly, but is extremely important in maintaining the integrity of the sampling method and to allow the computation of a response rate at the end of the survey. In these types of surveys only those individuals or households on the sample list should be approached for interview. The time of day when interviewing is conducted also has a major bearing on response rates.

For example, if a survey is directed at people who are economically active then commonsense suggests that attempts to interview them are more likely to more successful in the evening time rather than during the day.

Likewise time of day may not be a major factor if a survey is directed at people aged 65+ who will be more likely to be at home during the day.

PROVIDE AN INCENTIVE

Incentives can be a useful aid in gaining cooperation with a survey. These can be in the form of a monetary incentive either at the start or end of the interview, shopping vouchers, book vouchers or a promise to make a donation to charity.

AVOID USING 'IDENTIFIERS'

In relation to self-completion questionnaires always try and avoid using identifiers such as numbers on the questionnaire. People need to be reassured that their views will remain confidential and sometimes the use of identifiers in survey research can compromise this.

4.3.6
QUESTIONNAIRE DESIGN

"WHAT'S THE DIFFERENCE BETWEEN A 'SURVEY' AND A 'QUESTIONNAIRE'?"

The terms 'survey' and 'questionnaire' are quite often taken to mean the same thing. However, for the purposes of this tool kit, the term 'survey' refers to the whole exercise of collecting data whereas the term 'questionnaire' refers to actual tool or instrument used to collect the information needed (i.e. a set of ordered questions for the respondent to answer).

COMMON ELEMENTS

Regardless of which type of survey is used, there are a number of common elements: questionnaires seek direct answers rather than generating discussion; they are usually text based; questionnaires are normally designed to be answered by individuals; questions are generally pre-formulated and fixed; questions are structured in a logical sequence; respondents will normally choose their answers from a number of predefined answer categories by ticking boxes or circling categories; the questionnaire may contain some open questions to capture qualitative information; and, the results from the questionnaire are normally statistically based.

DESIGNING QUESTIONS

Always use pre-existing information to write questions. This can be supported by surveys which have already been carried out. Think about using questions which have been used in national or international surveys which will allow you to compare your findings.

For example, questions on the strength of community or the health status of a community can be quite powerful when used in local surveys and then compared against national and international levels.

Don't reinvent the wheel. Re-use questions which have performed well in the past. This will not only save time and effort, but if questions are exactly the same as questions in national surveys the likelihood is that these questions have already been tried and tested.

Begin by writing down the information you need, not the question you want ask e.g. 'I need to think about what people think about a new service' rather than 'what do you think of this new service'. The latter is a very broad question which will provide a great deal of open text but the former acts as a stimulus for thinking about the more detailed closed questions you might ask.

Be consistent: although varying question styles throughout a questionnaire keeps respondents 'on their toes', try to be consistent in questioning style e.g. if respondents are being asked to rate their responses from 1 to 5, don't suddenly change this to 1 to 10 in later questions.

Try and put yourself in the place of the respondent and remember you will not be there to help clarify the question when a respondent is answering it. This is where running a pilot survey will help to iron out any likely problems.

Validity is a statistical concept which is helpful to understand if the statistical results from a survey are to stand up to scrutiny. Validity is concerned with the conclusions that are generated from a piece of research. Put simply, validity is a measurement of how much the questionnaire correctly measures what it is supposed to measure.

Ensuring that the sample being used is representative of the population or target group will increase the validity of the survey but there are several ways to make sure that the questionnaire itself is as valid as possible: try and make sure the questions are clear and unambiguous; try and ensure that questions follow a logical sequence and relate to each other in a consistent way; and, use trials, pilots and other feedback to ensure that respondents understand the questions and the route through them.

Think about 'funneling' the questions which simply means asking the less sensitive questions at the start of the questionnaire and the more sensitive questions at the end of the questionnaire.

DIFFERENT TYPES OF QUESTIONS

At the most basic level, questions can be categorised into two types: closed questions and open questions.

Closed questions are followed by a list of answers with respondents prompted to choose from, or to rank or rate. These types of questions generate quantitative data which lends itself to statistical analysis and reporting. These questions tend to be easier and less time-consuming for respondents to answer. On the downside they force respondents to choose a particular response category.

Open questions ask respondent to provide information by writing their own answer. These questions generate qualitative data. The key advantage is that open questions allow respondents to give their response the way they want, in a way that suits them. These questions also require less time at the design stage and can be very useful when piloting the questionnaire.

The main downside is that open questions rarely provide valid statistical data and that they are heavily text based which meaning that analysis takes more time to interpret and aggregate. Note that time spent developing an open question into a closed question will save a lot of time at the analysis and reporting stage.

EXAMPLES OF CLOSED QUESTIONS

SINGLE ANSWER
Respondents tick or circle one answer from a list: agree / disagree; yes / no; male / female etc;

SCALED QUESTIONS
Respondents select a single answer on scale e.g. 'Overall I am satisfied with the service provided: strongly agree; agree; neither agree nor disagree; disagree; strongly disagree';

MULTIPLE ANSWER
Respondents can select more than one item on a list: 'Have you used any of the following products? (tick as many as appropriate — followed by a list of products).

RATING
Respondents are asked to rate items in a list by scoring them: 'Rate each of the following aspects of service from 1 to 10 (where 10 is the highest score and 1 is the lowest).

RANKING
Respondents are asked to rank items in order of importance (e.g. rank the following service provided by government in order of importance (1 is the most important: 5 is the least important).

EXAMPLES OF OPEN QUESTIONS

FULL OPEN
Respondent can enter free text responses (e.g. Please say why you are dissatisfied with this aspect of service'.

GUIDED OPEN:
Open questions which guide or limit the answers to make it easier to analyse responses (Please list what you believe to be the single most important thing that will improve service).

OPEN NUMERICAL
Respondents are asked to enter a number into a box (e.g. how many times have you used this service in the last 12 months).

QUESTIONNAIRE ROUTING, LAYOUT AND DESIGN

Just as important as question wording is the way questions are laid out, and the ease with which respondents can chart a logical route through them.

> **At the most basic level, questions can be categorised into two types: closed questions and open questions.**

SEQUENCE

Try and make it as easy as possible for respondent to navigate their way through the questionnaire. It should be relatively easy for respondents to answer the first set of questions which relate to easy demographic questions such as age and sex.

Avoid opening questions that are challenging and put an unnecessary burden on the respondent to answer. If challenging questions need to be asked put them at the end of the questionnaire when it is more likely that a rapport will have been established with the respondent and some level of trust has been built.

Some general points include: ask closed questions before open questions; ask questions about more general information before questions about more detailed information (use a 'drill down' technique); respondents will have the answer to the previous question in mind when they begin to answer the next one, so try and group similar questions to allow comparison or when a completely different question is being asked signal a change in emphasis (e.g. with a new heading section); and, always consider an question at the end of a section to pick up any other points respondents may wish to make.

FILTERS AND FUNNELS

A filter is a question which identifies a subset of respondents who may then be asked different questions from others in the survey. An example might be 'Have you used this service? (followed by a tick box yes/no). If yes is answered, then respondents can be asked about their experience of the service.

Funneling uses a series of filter questions to identify a particular subset of respondents that you may wish to target questions at. An example may be 'Have you been a victim of crime in the last 12 months? (yes/no). Those answering 'yes' may be asked if it was their home, office or vehicle that was burgled. If those who have had their home burgled is of interest then these respondents may be asked about their experience of dealing with the police with the others filtered out. When designing filters/funnels, make sure that filtered/funneled groups are brought back to the next common question by using a signpost. If the questionnaire contains a large number of questions for a filtered / funneled group, consider splitting the questionnaire and sending a separate one to the filtered group.

BALANCE

A good questionnaire will strike a balance between open and closed questions, with more emphasis on the latter if statistical information is required. If the final questionnaire is made up of mostly open questions then it may be worth considering using more qualitative methods to get the information required.

PILOTING

Piloting a questionnaire is extremely valuable. It will typically yield a variety of important insights, including:

- The number and variety of answers that are possible

- Whether respondents typically give more than one answer in response to a set of specific categories i.e., you will learn whether or not the set of answer categories you have selected are/are not mutually exclusive.

- What questions were not answered. It is highly beneficial to be aware of this. It gives you an opportunity to re-design such question before the main survey so as to improve your response rates. During the pilot phase in particular, always try and elicit an answer of some kind to each question – even if the respondent declines to answer a particular question, see if they will offer you a reason for this so you can get some insight into how you might adjust the question.

WORDING

Respondents must have a clear understanding of what is meant by a question and for this reason the use of jargon or overly technical language should be avoided.

USE SIMPLE WORDS
All respondents should be able to understand the questions (e.g. don't use the word 'regularly' if you can use the word 'often').

AMBIGUITY
Avoid using words and phrases which can be misunderstood by different groups of respondents (e.g. 'community' – does this mean a geographical area, neighbourhood, race, religion etc);

JARGON
Unless you are sure that all respondents understand the jargon, don't use it. Also be wary of using initials/acronyms.

LANGUAGE: AVOID LONG AND COMPLICATED QUESTIONS
As a general rule, questions should never be more than 20 words long. Make use of headings to set the context.

USE THE ACTIVE VOICE
For example, "Did you make a complaint this year?" rather than "Was a complaint made this year?."

AVOID LEADING QUESTIONS
which may make assumptions, for example: "How much will prices go up next year?" rather than "Do you think prices will go up next year?."

CLARITY

PAY ATTENTION TO DETAIL
Remember that a small error or spelling mistake can alter the focus of a question.

AVOID DOUBLE-BARRELLED QUESTIONS
For example, "Do you read newspapers and magazines?". Consider that someone might read newspapers but not magazines.

AVOID DOUBLE NEGATIVES
For example, respondents are asked to answer yes or no to the statement "I don't take exercise."

POSITIVE AND NEGATIVE STATEMENTS
When writing attitudinal statements (where respondents agree or disagree with the statements) mix positive and negative statements so that you show no bias.

Do this logically by mixing positive and negative statements in pairs in a set of attitude questions. Seeking the same information from two opposed attitude statements (so that a consistent respondent will answer positively to one statement and negatively to the other) will also help to identify 'straight-liners' i.e. those who complete a questionnaire by ticking the same boxes without considering the answer.

DON'T OVER-TAX MEMORIES
Most people are only able to remember recent events. Avoid questions which ask what they were doing months and years ago.

AVOID HEARSAY QUESTIONS
For example, "What do people in your area feel about health services?"

MAKE IT AS EASY AS POSSIBLE FOR THE RESPONDENT TO ANSWER ACCURATELY
This is sometimes called 'closing the question down'. Basically, you are trying to use information from other sources to enable the respondent to answer accurately. This can be achieved by considering if the information you need is fact or opinion. If fact, this is likely

to be easier if designed as a closed question. If an opinion is being sought the temptation may be to ask this as an open question. However, it is possible to devise a set of attitudinal statements and ask respondents if they agree or disagree with each statement. Try and get as much information as possible when 'closing a question down'. For example, instead of asking if you smoke (yes/no) the response categories could be changed to (yes, currently smoke; no, ex-smoker; no, never smoked).

SCALES

Many questionnaires used scaled questions and it is important to make sure that scales used are relevant and valid. Scales can be numeric (where the respondent is asked to circle a number) or they may be made up of a set of boxes for respondent to tick one (e.g. very likely; likely; unlikely; very unlikely) – these are known as semantic anchors.

SEMANTIC ANCHORS MUCH WORK IN A LOGICAL SEQUENCE

(e.g. Strongly agree; agree; neither; disagree; strongly disagree) and must make sense in the context of the question and respondent experience.

Also consider how many points should be used on a scale. Some researchers favour 5 points whereas others favour 10 points which can offer the option of identifying subtle differences between different groups of respondents. When considering how many points to use think about what the genuine differences are between points (e.g. is there likely to be a difference between strongly disagree and agree? Also think about how the information will be analysed (e.g. will particular categories be combined to form a single category such as 'strongly agree' and 'agree').

When measuring attitudes the Likert Scale is often used where respondents are asked to rate the level at which they agree or disagree with a given statement (e.g. there is a strong sense of community in my local area [strongly agree; agree; neither agree nor disagree; disagree; strongly disagree].

RATING AND RANKING

Both of these types of questions are related, in that they present the respondent with a list of items to be compared and scored using a limited numeric scale.

With rating, each item or question is scored individually and it is possible to give two items the same score. Nonetheless respondents will usually have the list of items in their mind which they are being asked to rate and so some comparison will take place.

When respondents are asked to rank questions they are forced to put them in order with no option to award equal status to two or more items.

GENERAL POINTS

Always consider including 'don't know', 'can't remember', 'not applicable' and 'refused' as answer categories.

It is good practice to include an 'Other' option after a closed list (with a space to allow respondent to write their response).

Closed questions can often be followed by a short open response asking respondents to qualify their answer (e.g. please say why you are satisfied with this service).

When conducting subgroup analysis the application of different statistical tests will help establish if the observed differences between different groups are statistically significant.

4.3.7
DATA HANDLING AND ANALYSIS

If the survey has been conducted using pen and paper the data from the questionnaires will need to be entered into a spreadsheet before analysis. When the data is input into the spreadsheet, the first task is to review the data to make sure that it is logically correct and that no data is missing.

If some problems are identified then simply refer back to the hardcopy questionnaire to fix the problem. The survey questionnaire may have also collected qualitative data which needs to be coded or categorized into particular themes. This involves manually reviewing each qualitative response and giving each new theme or idea you encounter a number. This is then entered into the spreadsheet.

By processing all of the qualitative comments in this way, you can see the nature and scale of the various themes / ideas that have recurred.
A number of options exist for analyzing survey data including Microsoft Excel and the dedicated statistical software programs such as SPSS and SNAP. Both SPSS and SNAP tend to be relatively

expensive and will require an annual user licence.
Before analysing the survey data, it is always good practice to first review the profile of the sample that your participation exercise has generated. This is done by reviewing the sample profile in terms of age and gender etc and then comparing this with what you know about the population from which it was drawn.

At this point, you should be checking to see if there is any bias in the sample (e.g. are there more men than women represented in the sample, or is there a greater proportion of older respondents in the sample compared with the population etc).

If you are satisfied that there is no bias in the sample then you can proceed to data analysis. If there is bias in the sample then you may need to apply a statistical weighting procedure to correct for this.

Normally, the first thing to do when analysing data is to run a set of frequencies to find out the response to each question. This is followed by running a set of crosstabulations to find out how particular groups of respondents

answered questions compared with other groups (e.g. comparing the responses of men and women or people of different age groups).

When conducting subgroup analysis the application of different statistical tests will help establish if the observed differences between different groups are statistically significant. Such statistical tests include chi-square, ANOVA and Regression Analysis.

4.4 QUALITATIVE METHODS
4.4.1 WHAT'S THAT?

Qualitative research explores attitudes, behaviour and experiences through methods such as interviews or group discussions. It strives to get an in-depth opinion from participants.

Since it is attitudes, behaviour and experiences which are important, fewer people may take part in the research, but the contact with each of these people tends to be longer per person than with quantitative research.

4.4.2 WIDELY USED QUALITATIVE TECHNIQUES

Within this section, we will look three qualitative techniques that are well-established and are widely used. These include:

• Interviews;

• Focus Groups; and,

• Case Studies.

However, before we look at the individual methods there are some general points about qualitative research that are worth noting.

4.4.3 SOME GENERAL POINTS: WHO SHOULD TAKE PART IN QUALITATIVE RESEARCH?

Unlike quantitative research, there is no upper or lower limit on the number of participants you might choose to involve in qualitative research.

However, good practice suggests that the qualitative approach is most appropriate where there is clear need to have a detailed discussion about a range of specific issues with a particular participant or segment of participants with a particular responsibility or perspective and where this responsibility or perspective is likely to be distinctive from/ potentially conflict with the views of others.

HOW DO I GO ABOUT ANALYSING THE FEEDBACK?

At a practical level, the way in which qualitative information is analysed is typically governed by three considerations. You need to decide to what extent these apply to your participation exercise. These are:

• The level of detail required;

• The time available;

• The resources available (money and skilled staff).

There are many different methods that can be used to analyse qualitative data.

However, for most purposes, a method called 'content analysis' is usually sufficient. Content analysis involves analysing documents, text, or speech to find out what themes emerge. For example, what do people talk about the most? See how themes relate to each other.

The goal is to detect discrete explicit or hidden emphases that are relevant to your particular participant exercise.

When you are doing this, it is therefore essential to refer back to the terms of reference for the participation exercise to ensure that you are extracting the points of greatest relevance from the feedback.

Who should take part in qualitative research?

Unlike quantitative research, there is no upper or lower limit on the number of participants you might choose to involve in qualitative research.

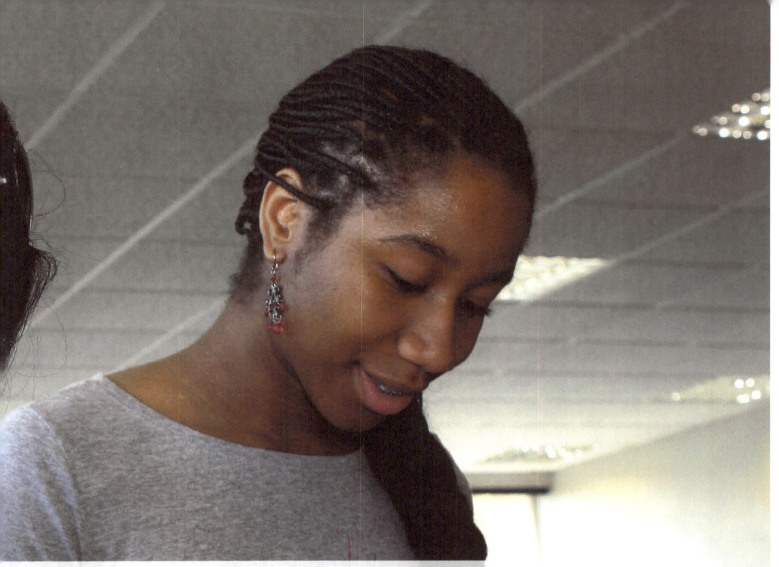

In practice, there are different ways in which content analysis can be done. Your choice of approach will depend on the level of detail you require and the time and skills you have available.

It is possible to code your interview findings into specialised computer programs. These programs do not analyse the data for you as such but rather help you format the data so that you can perform the analysis more easily.

However, computer programs are not essential and many experienced qualitative researchers manage perfectly well simply by using word processors or cutting out key phrases from the transcripts and arranging them in theme.

Indeed, the insight you gain by working intimately with the feedback, until you fully understand what it contains, is a real asset in itself, and is often the key to fully understanding the priorities within the feedback.

In some cases, specialised software, with its insistence that the data be entered and formatted in a particular way, can actually take more time and not necessarily add commensurate value to the insight you obtain.

HOW MUCH WILL IT COST?

Direct costs will arise where travel is required to reach a participant, when venues and hospitality are required and/or where a participant has to be incentivised to take part.

It is normally accepted that an explicit incentive is not required if the participant could reasonably to be expected to participate as part of their everyday role.

For example, a public worker would not normally be expected to be incentivised to take part in interviews during their normal working hours that pertain directly to their role as a public worker.

Direct costs will arise where travel is required to reach a participant, when venues and hospitality are required and/or where a participant has to be incentivised to take part. It is normally acceptable that an incentive is not required.

However, other participants, e.g. users, for whom a request for participation in an interview, focus group, case study etc. is likely to be competing with their leisure time, may need to be incentivised to take part.

The nature and value of the incentive needs to be given careful consideration so that it is both appropriate and likely to be valued by the participant, thereby maximising the chances of their engaging.

DO WE NEED FURTHER SKILLS/EQUIPMENT TO CARRY OUT QUALITATIVE RESEARCH?

In general, the individuals involved in carrying out qualitative research need to possess some or all of the following skills, or be in a position to buy them in.

These may include:

• Project management skills;

• Developing discussion guides;

• Designing questions;

• Listening skills;

• Facilitation skills;

• Group work;

• Note taking;

• Time management;

• Voice recording; and,

• Development of transcripts.

Those involved in analysing the feedback would benefit from having skills and experience of one or more of the qualitative analysis techniques. If further specialist skills/equipment are needed to deploy any of the following qualitative methods, we highlight this in the appropriate section in the following pages.

PROFILE

MyHealth@Age Project

A participant studies a mobile device at a MyHealth@Age workshop in Newry, Northern Ireland.

MyHealth@Age is an innovative project, involving collaboration between health service providers, information and communication technology (ICT) companies and universities in Sweden, Norway and Northern Ireland, developing new products and services that offer older people mobile-phone based services for improved health, safety and well-being.

The MyHealth@Age project received European Union funding through the Northern Periphery Programme, an INTERREG IVB Transnational Programme.

The partners include:
Healthcare and welfare organisations - City of Luleå, Municipality of Boden, Norrbotten County Council, Social Welfare Department of Tromsø kommune and Southern Health and Social Care Trust Ulster.
Universities and research centres - Centre of Distance Spanning Healthcare at Luleå University of Technology, Norwegian Centre for Telemedicine at University Hospital of North Norway and University of Ulster.
Information and communication technology companies - Arctic Group, Blue Tree Services, IntelliWork AB, McElwaine SMART Technologies, Swarmteams, TeliaSonera and TietoEnator.

The project will create a new modular product platform that makes it possible to provide safety, prescribed self treatment and social network applications to elderly people based on each individual's specific needs and circumstances.

The project developed three concepts: a mobile safety alarm with wirelessly connected fall sensor, that includes functionality for older end-users, alarm centre staff and

New technologies that can help improve the health and safety of older people.

welfare assistance staff; prescribed healthcare that supports self-diagnosis measurements, medication support and secure messaging between patients and healthcare staff; and a social network to stimulate social contacts between older people.

MyHealth@Age keeps the needs of older people at the centre of its approach and works closely with them when designing products and services. This is critical to success as, whilst the recent generation of elderly people is more comfortable using Information and Communication Technology, it is still very important that the products are unobtrusive and fit naturally into daily life.

The project methodology uses the European Living Lab innovation model, with a collaboration of Public-Private-Civic Partnerships in which stakeholders work together to create new products, services, businesses and technologies in real life environments and virtual networks in multi-contextual spheres. This approach is multifaceted, in that it facilitates open and continuous multi-stakeholder and multi-disciplinary collaboration that originates from, and is validated by user needs.

The project uses a participatory design and participatory action research approach, where the user needs are specified and validated in a multi-stage co-creative design process. The design process is iterated using qualitative methods between the partners including: (1) the community of end users (older people and healthcare professionals); (2) the healthcare and welfare organisations; (3) the businesses and (4) the multidisciplinary academic researchers.

www.northernperiphery.eu

European Union
European Regional Development Fund

4.4.4 INTERVIEWS
What's an interview?

An interview is an exchange between a questioner (the interviewer) and one or more interviewees. The purpose is to probe the ideas of the interviewees about the topic under discussion.

There are two types of interviews, structured and unstructured. In structured interviewing there are a pre-determined set of questions and each interviewee is asked the same questions. The feedback from this is relatively easy to analyse.

In unstructured interviewing, the interviewee presents some initial guiding questions but there is no formal topic guide or pre-determined sequence to the discussion.

Within this format, the interviewer can move the exchange in any direction that may come up and consequently, unstructured interviewing is especially beneficial for exploring an issue in general terms.

However, because of the lack of structure, each interview tends to be different in format and content, which makes subsequent analysis much more complex, especially when collating feedback across a wide range of interviews.

WHOM SHOULD I INTERVIEW?

Typically, a participation exercise will involve a series of one to one interviews with the key players.

These interviews are opportunities to gain real insight into the nuances of the subject matter under investigation and help you navigate the 'terrain' of the participation exercise (practical or political or both) more easily.

Interviews are also highly appropriate where information of a sensitive nature is to be explored and/or where the interviewee is unlikely for whatever reason.

to feel comfortable openly sharing their views in a group discussion, E.g. commercial interests or fear of criticism.

Across your sample of key players, strive to ensure that you have captured as diverse a range of views and experiences as possible about the initiative under examination. It may help to think about, who is likely to be supportive, and who is likely to be critical and seek views from each segment.

HOW DO I CONDUCT AN INTERVIEW?

Interviews can be conducted face to face and when dealing with sensitive and complex subject matter, and/or when striving to develop relationships with key players within a participation exercise, this is normally the preferred approach. However, interviews can also be conducted by telephone or teleconferencing technology if the travel time or cost involved in a face to face cannot be justified by the level of insight or relationship building anticipated.

Whatever the approach, it is often very helpful for the interviewer to speak directly with the prospective interviewee, even on the phone, when setting up the date, time and arrangement for the interview. This gives you, the interviewer, the opportunity to outline the questions that will be asked whilst simultaneously giving the interviewee an opportunity to ask questions about the participation exercise and their role in it.

This exchange will help you to clarify whether or not they are the most appropriate person to interview (e.g. it is not uncommon for a different member of someone's team to be closer to the issues and hence be more appropriate to interview than the person first identified).

The interviewee needs to be clear from you on the arrangements and the time that will be involved.

You will also, typically, need to send them the agenda for the interview in advance, to help them prepare, unless you have specific reasons for wanting them to give you more spontaneous answers.

One to one interviews, whether face to face, telephone or teleconference-type technology can be recorded in a variety of ways (e.g. stenography, video recording, voice recording or written notes) if the interviewee is told in advance and gives their consent. (Any request for recording should be made clear at the time the interview is set up).

Video or voice recordings can be used either to create transcripts (from which the interview can later be analysed in detail) or can be treated as reference material, if as the interviewer, you opt to simply note the key points during the interview.

Whether you choose to do stenography or create video, voice recordings and/or transcripts will largely depend on the extent to which it is deemed important that you note everything that is mentioned during the interview or simply note the key points.

A further consideration is the time and cost involved in carrying out such recordings and, if required, producing the transcripts. When the date, time and arrangement for the interview has been set, it is good practice and usually more time efficient, if, a suitable number of days beforehand, interviewees are sent an advance notice (typically by email) summarising the background to the participation exercise and the agenda for the interview. This gives interviewees time to prepare which will usually help to enhance the level and quality of feedback you receive from them.

HOW LONG WILL IT TAKE?

Planning a small series of interviews (<10) and setting them up, takes typically a couple of person days to plan the agenda and set up the individual arrangements. A face to face interview or a teleconference interview can typically last an hour or so. Telephone interviews are typically shorter (the lack of visual feedback between interviewee and interviewer make it more difficult to sustain the level of engagement that is achievable in a face to face or teleconference context). Analysing the information typically takes at least twice as long as the interview itself.

STRENGTHS AND WEAKNESSES

- Interviews are good for depth of discussion and understanding specifics.

- They are helpful when you need to examine sensitive issues.

- However, relative to quantitative methods, interviews are expensive.

Hence the need to use them only with the key individuals required and only in relation to specific issues where the answers cannot be found by any other means.

4.4.5
WHAT'S A 'FOCUS GROUP'?

A focus group is an organised (usually recorded – voice and / or video) discussion with a selected group of individuals (typically 6 – 10) to gain information about their views and experiences of a specific topic(s) and to explore how these views are influenced by others in a group situation.

Whilst each focus group can have between 6 – 10 participants, experience suggests that focus groups with between six and eight participants work best.

An independent moderator sets the questions and facilitates the discussion. A further member of the staff may be present to support the moderator by taking notes.

Focus groups normally last about 90 - 120 minutes in total.

The purpose of a focus group is not to reach consensus on an issue but rather to explore the range of attitudes and views held about it.

WHO SHOULD TAKE PART IN THE FOCUS GROUPS?

Typically, participation exercises usually involve a series of focus groups with individuals selected for specific characteristics. For example, if you were interested in exploring the reaction of older men towards a possible new cancer therapy, you might set up focus groups as follows:

- Focus Group 1
  Males, over 65, social class ABC1, who have had cancer;

- Focus Group 2
  Males, over 65, social class ABC1, who have not had cancer;

- Focus Group 3
  Males, over 65, social class C2DE, who have had cancer;

- Focus Group 4
  Males, over 65, social class C2DE, who have not had cancer etc.

Such an arrangement would give you a range of views across social class and experience of cancer. Depending on where the new therapy was available, you may be interested in views of men living in rural areas compared with urban areas. And if so, you would add this into your selection criteria.

The specific characteristics of interest will vary depending on the particular issues you wish to examine in your participation exercise. This has implications for how you recruit for the focus groups.

The way in which you will identify focus group participants will vary depending on the subject under consideration and the questions you wish to pose. For example, you may wish to have focus groups of the general public, in which case a random sample would be appropriate. You may be interested in the views of people of a particular age and gender who live in a specific locality – in which case an on street recruitment in that locality could be used to generate your sample. In general, a stratified sample will enable you to achieve a balance of views.

For example, in some situations, you may need to listen to the views of people living in a certain geographical area. In this case, you could send recruiters door to door in that area to identify appropriate participants. In another participation exercise, you may need to listen to the views and experiences of people who have used a specific service. In this situation, you may have/be given access to a list of past/current service users from which you could identify potentially suitable candidates and then approach each of them directly to test if they would be willing to participate.

The number and range of focus groups you decide to run will depend on:

a. the diversity within the population/ segment you wish to engage with;

b. the extent to which that diversity is likely to affect the nature of the feedback you will receive from the participants (e.g. ask yourself, might people in rural areas have different opinions on this topic compared with people in urban areas? If so, you may need separate focus groups, if not, then you do not.)

c. Your timescale and budget.

HOW DO I DESIGN MY FOCUS GROUPS SO AS TO MAXIMISE INSIGHT?

Focus groups are normally used in combination with other methods to expand understanding around how a particular issue is being perceived/ experienced. They can be used in a number of ways, for example:

- As the first participation tool – to get an early insight into how people are thinking about a particular issue and to help identify the key themes for more detailed investigation – akin to a 'scoping' tool;

- During a participation process – to improve understanding of how an issue is being thought about; and,

- After other participation techniques e.g. a survey have been conducted – to help understand why the findings were as they were.

It is quite common for participation exercises to carefully construct focus groups so that segments with possibly very different points of view are in different groups e.g. men who have had cancer, men who have not. However, for certain types of discussions, you may wish to deliberately mix the composition of the groups to stimulate an exchange of potentially diverse and divergent views (e.g. a focus groups with business leaders and academics).

These latter groups often require very experienced facilitators and this needs to be borne in mind when designing the schedule for focus groups.

The way in which you will identify focus group participants will vary depending on the subject under consideration and the questions you wish to pose. For example, you may wish to have focus groups of the general public, in which case a random sample would be appropriate.

You may be interested in the views of people of a particular age and gender who live in a specific locality – in which case an on street recruitment in that locality could be used to generate your sample. In general, a stratified sample will enable you to achieve a balance of views.

For each focus group, always recruit more participants than 8 ('10 for 8' is a widely used arrangement) It is quite common for participants who have confirmed they are coming to drop out at the last minute for any number of reasons. You will need a list of reserves whom you can call on at the last minute if necessary.

HOW DO I ACTUALLY CONDUCT A FOCUS GROUP?

Again, as with an interview, you will need to explain to each participant the reason for the focus group, their role in it, the arrangements (date, time, venue), the confidential nature of their contribution, details of any incentive they will receive for taking part and how this will be administered.

Having explained this to them at the time of recruitment, it is also good practice to provide this in writing, ideally at the time of recruitment or immediately afterwards in writing (email or letter).

The topics for discussion in the focus group need to be aligned directly with the terms of reference for the participation exercise – be clear what you want to learn from the focus group.

Work with your colleagues to explore and agree what specific questions should be asked. Structure your topics guide so that the easy to answer questions are at the start and the more complex issues appear later on.

Assign an approximate time allocation for each question that reflects the importance of that topic in the context of the terms of reference overall. Also, make sure that the questions are posed in simple, conversational language and are open-ended as far as possible. This will help participants to feel at ease and will also facilitate a wide range of possible answers to come forth.

Given that you have around 120 minutes in total in a focus group, you need to manage the time available very carefully. Allow around 10 minutes for introductions and ground rules and about 5 minutes for closing and summing up.

With just over 100 minutes left, you may be tempted to try to squash in a lot of questions – resist this! One of the keys to an effective focus group is to choose a small number of questions (typically around 6 – 8) that are critical to your participation exercise and focus on gaining an in-depth insight into partcipants' views on these.

It is highly beneficial to pilot these questions with a few colleagues beforehand to test how they are interpreted and to check that they are addressing the issues intended.

A further practical point is to choose venues for the focus groups that are convenient, accessible and where participants will feel safe and comfortable in.

The layout you choose for the focus group should, ideally, reflect the preferences of the participants and the subject matter under discussion. Some participants will be more comfortable in a formal set up (e.g. with desks etc), others may prefer an informal setting (low seating coffee tables etc.) or chairs in a semi-circle.

It is normal practice to provide participants with modest hospitality (e.g. tea/coffee etc) on arrival. This is not simply a courtesy is also an important opportunity to build rapport between the moderator and the participants and the participants themselves – thereby helping to maximise the 'gelling' of the group and so creating the conditions whereby honest and fulsome feedback is more likely to be maximised.

To record the feedback from focus groups, the proceedings can, with permission from the participants, be voice recorded, videoed and/or notes taken.

WHAT OTHER WAYS ARE THERE TO STIMULATE FEEDBACK IN A FOCUS GROUP?

Whilst most focus groups major on talking and listening, there are other ways in which participants can be supported to share their views. This can range from inviting them to depict their views by way of a picture or cartoon, select of an image (picture or photo which best represents their views) or an imaginary scale.

HOW LONG DO FOCUS GROUPS TAKE TO DO SET UP, CONDUCT AND ANALYSE?

Planning a small series of focus groups (say 4) and setting them up, takes typically a couple of person days to plan the agenda, recruit the participants and set up the arrangements. Each focus group typically takes about 2 hours to conduct. However, as with interviews, analysing the information typically takes at least twice as long as the focus group itself.

HOW MUCH WILL IT COST?

Direct costs can arise in terms of recruiting the participants, venue hire, hospitality for the participants, and, if appropriate, incentives for the participants.

STRENGTHS AND WEAKNESSES

• Unlike one to one interviews, focus groups potentially expose the participants to a wide range of views on specific subjects and, hence, can be helpful in examining complex issues in more detail.

• Unlike large meetings, with a small number of attendees (6 – 8 typically), most participants can be enabled to have the confidence and opportunity to have their say and this rich exchange of views is very beneficial in exploring multi-faceted issues.

• However, effective focus groups need to be facilitated by experienced personnel otherwise it can, on occasions, be difficult to separate the view of the group from the view of a few vocal individuals.

• In addition, the nature of the feedback from focus groups is qualitative and hence it cannot have statistical validity.

4.4.6 CASE STUDIES

WHAT'S A 'CASE STUDY'?

A case study is a dedicated study of a specific individual or a specific context for the purpose of understanding a larger group of similar entities.

WHAT SHOULD I PUT IN A CASE STUDY?

There are no strict rules about how you select the subject of your case study. In the context of participation exercises, we suggest that the individual or context you choose for your case study should be one that adds to the body of knowledge about the key questions which your participation exercise seeks to answer.

HOW DO I COLLECT THE INFORMATION I NEED FOR A CASE STUDY?

In a case study, you are typically seeking to understand what determined 'success' or 'failure' in a particular situation There is no single way to do this and a combination of methods (e.g., interviews –structured and/or unstructured, direct observation, review of literature, surveys, focus groups etc) are often used.

Writing a good case study is a little bit like writing a detective story. You need to write it in such a way as to keep your audience interested. This typically means presenting key facts (for context), key challenges, how these were addressed and what has been learned form this. In a way, you are trying to take the reader through the same thought processes and challenges that you experienced as the researcher.

The three basic processes in compiling a case study are:

- Research;
- Analysis;
- Write up.

RESEARCH

This phase typically involves a combination of:

- Desk based research on your chosen subject – to find out more about the facts and the specific issues in that context;

- Interviews with/surveys/focus groups etc. with key stakeholders who can expand your understanding of the facts and the issues.

ANALYSIS

This phase typically involves sifting through the information you have collected to select the pieces that are most relevant to the key issue about this case study.

There is no prescribed way of doing this. Often it helps to work with a group of colleagues when doing this, as this enables you to challenge one another, in a constructive way, on what to include or exclude.

The goal is to identify the minimum set of information a reader will need to understand the key points you wish to make.

WRITE UP

One of the most helpful ways to write up a case study is to treat it like a puzzle. Start off by posing a question or a problem that the reader is invited to explore, and then lead the reader, piece by piece, to 'reveal' the findings and learning from your case study. Whilst there is no specific format for writing a case study, it is generally helpful to consider having an introductory section, a section on the key issues, followed by sections on what was done/tried, what resulted from this, what was learned, and finally, your conclusions from all of this.

There are no fixed timescales for the compilation of a case study. Much depends on how much data already exists, what further research you need to do and the level of detail you wish to include in the case study.

HOW DO I KNOW IF MY CASE STUDY IS RELIABLE?

There is no single way to test the reliability of a case study. Given that a case study is intentionally composed of a mixture of data sets, the reliability of the case study will be determined by the underlying quality of the data sets you use and the objectivity of the interpretation you apply to them. One practical way to test the reliability of your case study – and whether all of the elements 'work' together i.e. whether it is clear and coherent – is to ask those who contributed to it and your Steering Group to critique it.

HOW LONG DOES IT TAKE TO PRODUCE A CASE STUDY?

There are no fixed timescales for the compilation of a case study. Much depends on how much data already exists, what further research (e.g. surveys, interviews, focus groups etc) you need to do and the level of detail you wish to include in the case study. The whole process could take hours, days or weeks. Ultimately, the investment you make in any case study will, in part be determined by, the diversity and complexity of the issues under examination within your participation exercise and the extent to which the understanding of this subject matter is facilitated when it is presented as a composite (i.e. as a 'story' with different parts.

HOW MUCH WILL IT COST?

The breadth, depth and complexity of a case studies varies, Consequently, it is not possible to assign a fixed cost of the production of a case study. The cost of compiling a case study could be modest if it only involves desk research. However, direct costs can arise if further participation is required (e.g. surveys, interviews, focus groups etc).

DO WE NEED ANY ADDITIONAL SKILLS?

The individuals involved in compiling case studies would benefit from having (or buying in) skills in analysing quantitative and qualitative research, and if required, conducting surveys, interviews and focus groups.

STRENGTHS AND WEAKNESSES

• They can provide depth of understanding around a particular situation/context.

• They bring together different types of evidence to improve understanding about what is happening.

• They can, if well designed, yield insight into how similar challenges might be addressed elsewhere.

• However, there is no official standard or format for a case study so the quality and usefulness of the case study is largely determined by the skills and creativity of the author(s).

• In addition, the findings from the case study may be difficult to generalise because the characteristics of the context chosen for examination was uncommon in some way(s);

• Finally, it can be time consuming and inefficient to gather data sets which are later sifted out because, whilst they provide a level of background information, they are not used within the final case study itself.

4.5 MIXED METHODS
What's a 'mixed' method?
A mixed method is one that engages participants using elements of the quantitive and qualitative approaches within a single method.

Why would I choose to use a mixed method?

A mixed method is especially effective at overcoming the limitations of group discussions where it can sometimes be very difficult to separate the group's view from the views of any specific participant, and to capture the views of those who may be reluctant to be identified when expressing their views openly in a group setting.

WHAT DOES IT INVOLVE?

One example of a mixed method, which we will explore here, is an electronic audience response system. This specialised software and hardware involves each participant being issued with a voting device that communicates with a receiving device. In the case of a conventional group discussion, the participants with the voting devices and the receiving device are in the same room. However, similar group discussions could take place via teleconferencing and the voting could take place via the internet.

Using this technology, one can 'programme' multiple choice questions or statements into the audience response system and display these to the group.

The participants can them be invited to indicate their own view on these statements or questions by using the number pad e.g. 1=Agree Strongly, 2=Agree, 3=Neutral, 4=Disagree, 5=Disagree strongly etc. In this way, the views of each participant are captured quantitatively.

However, the 'voting' in each case can be preceded by a group discussion on the various aspects of the question/statement under review. In this way, unlike a survey where each person answers without reference to others, the participant has an opportunity to listen to, influence and be influenced by the thinking of others before the views of each participant are then captured.

Most technology of this type offers a range of features including displaying the results of the voting (as charts), and production of

various reports on the data generated, e.g. to look at the demographics of the responses.

Some such systems offer the facility to suppress the display of charts and still capture the data in the background. This can be useful when handling sensitive issues.

In addition, most systems offer the facility to track the responses according to key characteristics (that you have predefined) or, alternatively, allow participants to respond completely anonymously.

HOW DO I KNOW IF THE FEEDBACK FROM SUCH SESSIONS RELIABLE?

Using such technology creates an immediate opportunity for triangulation – one can see straight away what views are being expressed by the group as it discusses and explores a topic (i.e. the qualitative dimension) compared with how participants vote on key issues when they are given the opportunity (i.e. the quantitative dimension).

HOW LONG DOES IT TAKE TO SET UP A MIXED SESSION?

It will take time to recruit the various participants for the group discussion and voting session. The time required will depend on many factors including the ease of access to a suitable sample of contacts and the availability of suitable venues etc.

HOW MUCH DOES IT COST TO SET UP AND RUN A MIXED SESSION LIKE THE ONE DESCRIBED?

The specialised software and hardware – and the training involved in how to use it - will cost money. These costs can be considerable.

DO I NEED ANY ADDITIONAL SKILLS?

As well as acquiring the technical skills to use the specialised software and hardware, the key skill is participation event design – i.e. knowing where and how to position the key aspects of qualitative and quantitative research within the overall event, knowing how to ask the questions which will yield insight into the specific issues of interest in your participation exercise.

STRENGTHS AND WEAKNESSES

• Mixed methods overcome some of the key issues associated with conventional group work i.e. separating the view of an individual view from that of the group.

• However, the specialised software and hardware – either to buy outright or buy in (as a service) can be expensive.

Mixed methods can be useful to overcome some key issues concerning group activities but specialised software and hardware - if needed - can be very expensive.

4.6 EMERGING METHODS
4.6.1 WHAT'S NEW?

Information technology is increasingly being used to support and enhance participation exercises. The precise ways in which it is being used are changing on a daily basis. What is clear is that information technology, and the internet in particular, are being used to support new forms of participation that involving linking together large numbers of (often geographically disparate) people, to converse. The use of these technologies is becoming more highly popular and this trend looks set to increase extensively in future.

This explosion in the use of information technology and the internet is having major implications for those designing and conducting participation exercises.

Consequently, it is important for those with such responsibility to be aware of the main methods that are emerging, how they can be used and their key strengths and weaknesses. The main methods we will look at here are 'virtual focus groups', panels and social media.

4.6.2
VIRTUAL FOCUS GROUPS

WHAT'S A 'VIRTUAL FOCUS GROUP'?

A 'virtual focus group', shares many of the features of a conventional focus group. Like a conventional focus group, it is an organised discussion with a selected group of individuals (typically 6 – 10) to gain information about their views and experiences of a specific topic(s) and to explore how these views are influenced by others in a group situation. As with a conventional focus group, the moderator sets the questions and the purpose is not to reach consensus on an issue but rather to explore the range of attitudes and views held about it.

However, the key difference between virtual focus groups and conventional focus groups is that the moderator is not physically present in the same room as the participants and that the participants are not in the same room. The moderator and each of the participants are often geographically dispersed (typically because coming together as a physical focus group would be impractical because of time, cost, other factors e.g. home working, disability, live in different time zones).

Under this arrangement, all of the communication – between the moderator and the participants and the participants and one another - is done by inputting text asynchronously (i.e. each participant types in their responses to the questions at a different time) on line over the internet using 'chat room' style technology.

In this situation, participants enter their responses over a much longer period (e.g. say 48 hours to a week, compared with a 2 hour conventional focus group).

In this context, the role of the moderator is less interventionist and less directive than in a conventional focus group. Virtual listening and prompting with probes and extra questions replaces the steering role of the face to face moderator.

This approach creates a distinctly different dynamic for interaction which can be beneficial or unhelpful depending on a range of factors including the ICT skills of the participants, and the sensitivity of the subject matter under discussion.

WHO SHOULD I INVITE TO TAKE PART IN A VIRTUAL FOCUS GROUP?

How you decide the profile of the participants within each focus group and how you settle on a number of focus groups overall will be done on the same basis as for conventional focus groups. A key consideration however, will be ensuring that the participants are sufficiently confident and competent in using the specific information technology you choose for the interaction.

HOW DO I COLLECT THE FEEDBACK FROM A VIRTUAL FOCUS GROUP?

Virtual focus groups can be used in the same sorts of ways as conventional focus groups i.e. in combination with other methods to expand understanding around how a particular issue is being perceived/experienced. Again, as with conventional focus groups, they can be used in a number of ways, for example:

• As the first participation tool;
• During a participation process; and,
• After other participation techniques to help understand why the findings were as they were.

Like conventional focus groups, always recruit more participants than 8 ('10 for 8' is a widely used arrangement). It is quite common for participants who have confirmed they will participate to drop out at the last minute for any number of reasons. You will need a list of reserves whom you can call on at the last minute if necessary.

Again, as with conventional focus groups, you will need to explain to each participant the reason for the focus group, their role in it, the arrangements (date, time, venue), the confidential nature of their contribution, details of any incentive they will receive for taking part and how this will be administered.

"As with conventional focus groups, one of the keys to an effective virtual focus group is to choose a small number of questions (typically around 6 – 8) that are critical to your participation exercise and focus on gaining an in-depth insight into participants' views on these. It is highly beneficial to pilot these questions with a few colleagues beforehand to test how they are interpreted and to check that they are addressing the issues intended."

Having explained this to them at the time of recruitment, it is also good practice to provide this in writing, ideally at the time of recruitment or immediately afterwards in writing (email or letter).

The topics for discussion in the focus group need to be aligned directly with the terms of reference for the participation exercise – be clear what you want to learn from the focus group.

Again, work with your colleagues to explore and agree what specific questions should be asked. Structure your topics guide so that the easy to answer questions are at the start and the more complex issues appear later on.

Also, make sure that the questions are posed in simple, conversational language and are open-ended as far as possible. This will help participants to feel at ease and will also facilitate a wide range of possible answers to come forth.

As with conventional focus groups, one of the keys to an effective virtual focus group is to choose a small number of questions (typically around 6 – 8) that are critical to your participation exercise and focus on gaining an in-depth insight into participants' views on these.

It is highly beneficial to pilot these questions with a few colleagues beforehand to test how they are

interpreted and to check that they are addressing the issues intended. A further practical point is to ensure to choose venues for the focus groups that are convenient, accessible and where participants will feel safe and comfortable in.

Since you do not have the opportunity to offer participants tea and coffee in a virtual focus group (at least, not using today's technology!), you will need to find other ways to build rapport between the moderator and the participants and the participants themselves.

This means that the way in which the participants are recruited and the way in which introductions are made is crucial. Whist anonymity is protected, it can be helpful to build rapport between the moderator and each participant over the phone at the time of recruitment.

In this context, the wording and tone of introductory text and the language used for each of the questions/probes are all crucial in setting the tone for the group overall.

In a virtual focus group, all of the responses are typed in by the participants and hence it is usually relatively straightforward to generate a full transcript of the exchanges and to drop them into other software (e.g. word processor or software for analysing qualitative responses).

HOW LONG DOES IT TAKE?

Given that the participants are geographically dispersed and may need some level of support to become confident with using the technology, planning a small series of virtual focus groups (say 4) and setting them up, takes typically several person days.

This involves planning the agenda, recruiting the participants and setting up the arrangements. Each focus group could span 48 hours to a week (or longer in some cases). Whilst transcripts are relatively easy to produce, analysing the information typically takes at least twice as long as the focus group itself.

HOW MUCH WILL IT COST?

Direct costs can arise in terms of recruiting the participants, the purchase or use of the specialist software, training for participants in the use of the software and incentives for the participants.

DO I NEED ANY ADDITIONAL SKILLS?

The individuals involved in carrying out virtual focus groups need all the generic skills identified at the start of this section. They also benefit from developing specialist skills in interacting with people using text as the only medium of communication.

This is a critical skill and one that could a) make or break the rapport within a virtual focus group and b) could disarm or inflame a 'difficult' participant(s).

STRENGTHS AND WEAKNESSES

Virtual focus groups share the advantages of conventional focus groups plus:

• They can facilitate exchanges between participants that might otherwise be difficult to access (e.g. because of disparate geography, disability etc). This is an asset from an equity point of view;

• The asynchronous format and the longer time period for responses allows flexibility for participation may encourage those who would be hesitant to respond in a conventional focus group to give their views. This format also gives participants more time to think about what they wish to say. This is especially important when considering sensitive issues;

• The fact that the moderator and the participants do not meet in person and the fact that the exchanges are all done through a secure, safe and anonymous environment, may help some participants feel more comfortable in giving their views (which could lead to better quality responses overall);

• Participants enter the discussion site with the specific intent of contributing their views on a particular topic. Consequently, there tends to considerable focus on the topic (minimal divergence) and so there is typically a more focused response to the questions; and,

• The fact that all the responses from participants are typed in on line makes it very easy to create transcripts. However, virtual focus group also share the disadvantages of conventional focus groups, plus:

• The moderator and the participants need to be competent and confident using information technology. Individuals with low or no level of IT literacy are likely to find this approach less accessible and could be at risk of marginalisation unless appropriately supported in a virtual focus group.

Training and support may also need to be provided. This could add cost to the participation exercises.

• It can be more challenging for the moderator to deal with very vocal participants when the only mechanism to communicate is typed text on line and the communication mode is asynchronous. The responses need to be carefully considered so as to have the appropriate effect whilst preserving the positive dynamic in the group.

• Related to this, whilst the anonymity afforded by virtual focus groups can be a tremendous asset in encouraging open and frank discussion, it can, on occasions, be misused by participants.

Some participants use this context to say things that they would not normally say, or even necessarily believe (e.g. something deliberately provocative).

Where this happens it can disrupt the dynamic of the group and become problematic for the moderator in terms of how to respond.

TRAIL researchers host an electronic town meeting on healthcare at the University of Ulster.

PROFILE

PARTERRE: eParticipation project

Electronic Participation Tools for Spatial Planning and Territorial Development

The PARTERRE project (supported by the European Commission under grant number 256244) aims to demonstrate and validate the business potential of novel e-participatory methods and tools for spatial and strategic planning at the European level, by leveraging the Electronic Town Meeting (eTM).

This was first introduced into Europe by Aventura Urbana srl and technically supported by the project's coordinating organisation, Regione Toscana. This is a deliberative democracy methodology and toolset combining the direct integration of small-group discussions with the advantages of electronic communication.

The Town Meeting is a form of structured participation in local government practised in the U.S. region of New England since colonial times, and in some Western States since at least the late 19th century. There, an entire community was invited by government officials to gather in a public place to formulate suggestions or provide feedback on specific policy issues. In its modern version - the Electronic Town Meeting – the use of ICT enables citizens to participate either directly, or indirectly or at least experimentally, in the upcoming debate.

The basic characteristics of an Electronic Town Meeting are the following: after information on a given topic has been provided, participants can express themselves individually within small groups, also known as "tables". Instant minutes of the tables discussions are kept by experienced facilitators - usually thanks to electronic means – with the aim of letting everyone's opinions and views emerge from the debate, without any attempt of formulating a unitary (or compromise) vision of that group. A central team (known as the "Theme Team"), composed by several domain experts,

collects and reviews the instant minutes, trying to cluster the issues emerged– with a special eye on conflicting, if not deviant, perspectives – and then provides rankings of statements which are finally submitted to a collective vote by all participants in the tables. To this purpose, every person is endowed with a remote control device.
One of the fundamental aims of the eTM is to assure the participants a high level of information on the central discussion topics allowing an "informed" debate at least along general lines.

With the eTM, not only are the citizens directly involved in a public decision making process, but the issues discussed are also prioritised in a way that is immediately visible to policy designers. Recently, the Regional Government of Tuscany has imported the Electronic Town Meeting into its own policy practice, by organising about ten initiatives of such a kind since 2006. Over time, this has led to the creation of an Open Source, web-based application for collective discussion and voting support, which is integrated with a streaming server to host the participants who may be localised remotely.

This application, together with dedicated training and assistance in its installation and configuration, is offered free of charge to all public authorities wanting to experiment an Electronic Town Meeting on premise. All necessary equipment includes a set of normal PC's for the discussion tables and the Theme Team, a video recording kit to support web streaming, a number of special remote controls that participants will use to express their votes, and a network hub connecting the site server with all individual tables. To participate in the Town Meetings remotely, users only need to access the Internet with their own PC or mobile device.

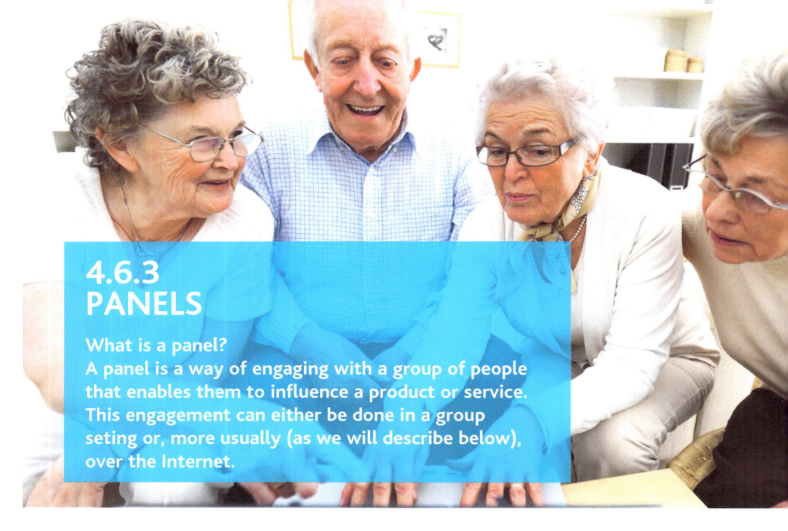

4.6.3
PANELS

What is a panel?
A panel is a way of engaging with a group of people that enables them to influence a product or service. This engagement can either be done in a group seting or, more usually (as we will describe below), over the Internet.

HOW TO I SET UP A 'PANEL'?

There are no hard and fast rules on the composition of a panel. However, a fundamental point is that you need to be clear on the purpose of your panel in relation to your particular participation exercise. Alongside this, you will want to think about things like:

• How much time and money can we afford to invest in this?
• What specific questions to we wish to put to this panel?
• What method(s) are the most appropriate to get feedback from panel members?
• How many participants should be involved?
• What specific characteristics are important to us?
• How will we recruit them?

Since there are no upper or lower limits on size, the size of the panel will be determined more by the time and budget you have to invest in establishing the panel and supporting it to participate.

From an economical point of view, it is useful to ascertain the minimum number and profile of participants you will need to ensure that that your findings are reliable and valid.

Panel members need to be recruited in much the same way that you would recruit for a focus group – you are looking for specific characteristics of interest e.g. age, gender, locality,

interests etc. which will inform your participation exercise. Panels can be composed of people drawn from the general population, or niche characteristics (e.g. voluntary sector providers providing support for older people in their homes).

All panels will need a level of induction and support to enable them to fully understand their role in the panel and the process through which they give their views. Depending on the size of panel, this could be done face to face or electronically.

HOW DO I GET FEEDBACK FROM A PANEL?

If you are using electronic surveys and/or virtual focus groups to communicate with your panel, you will need to ensure that all panel members are appropriately equipped, skilled and supported to do so. This usually costs money.

HOW DO I KNOW IF THE FEEDBACK FROM MY PANEL IS RELIABLE?

The reliability of survey data from panel members can be assessed using tests of the statistical significance of variations in the responses and by cross referencing the responses with the feedback obtained on the same subject via other methods of data collection from the same panel e.g. virtual focus groups.

"Panel members need to be recruited in much the same way that you would recruit for a focus group – you are looking for specific characteristics of interest e.g. age, gender, locality, interests etc. which will inform your participation exercise. Panels can be composed of people drawn from the general population, or niche characteristics. All panels will need a level of induction and support to enable them to fully understand their role in the panel and the process through which they give their views."

HOW LONG DOES IT TAKE TO SET UP A PANEL?

Setting up a panel can take several person days or weeks depending on its size and complexity. Also, panel members need to be replaced (if people drop out) and the entire membership refreshed periodically to ensure that the panel continues to be representative of the target group rather than 'professional panel members'! Time will need to be invested in preparing materials and the process for inducting new panel members and supporting them as the dialogue proceeds.

HOW MUCH DOES IT COST TO SET UP A PANEL?

All of the support and specialised equipment that panel members need will cost money. These costs can be considerable. However, the scale of the investment must be seen in the context of the value of the insight that is likely to be obtained from this process.

DO WE NEED ANY ADDITIONAL SKILLS?

The individuals involved in setting up panels would benefit from having (or buying in) skills in designing and conducting electronic surveys and virtual focus groups. Those involved in analysing the feedback would benefit from having skills and experience of one or more of the quantitative and qualitative analysis techniques.

STRENGTHS AND WEAKNESSES

• They enable specific groups of people (often geographically disparate) to participate and give their views;

• They can be constructed so that the feedback is statistically valid and reliable;

• Because of the anonymity, they can helpful when you need to examine sensitive issues.

• However, panels can be expensive to set up (given the requirement to invest in technology, and skill participants up and support them);

• In addition, the ongoing costs can be considerable as panel members need to be replaced and, on occasions, the entire panel membership needs to be refreshed;

• Finally, panels usually require a high degree of ICT literacy for participation which puts certain segments at risk of exclusion unless appropriate support is given.

4.6.4 WHAT'S SOCIAL MEDIA?

Social media is a generic term used to describe a range of Internet based technologies including social networking sites, photo and video creation and sharing, comment and message creation and sharing that place the power and connectivity of the Internet in the hands of everyday people.

The ease and scale of this connectivity mean that it is possible to communicate with and receive feedback from huge numbers of participants within seconds and at relatively low cost per interaction. The growth in the range of social media tools and their level of use amongst by individuals and groups/organisations has been massive in the recent years and this trend looks set to continue.

In the past, the Internet was used as a vehicle simply to share information. However, the emergence of social media means that the sharing of information can co-exist with the added facility to connect people to other people.

This facility to connect large numbers of people and their ideas — one with the other — easily, cheaply and in real time - creates the conditions within which relationships of various types and strengths can develop. In turn, this development of relationships between participants creates the potential for the emergence of strong, congruent, collective voices rather than weak, disparate, individual voices.

The latter effect can have a potent and immediate effect on the pace and direction of the debate on the issue/ initiative under consideration. This, in turn, has the potential to change the power dynamics, the expectations, and potentially the outcomes, of a particular participation exercise as it proceeds.

For example, the speed with which facts and opinions about unfolding events/ emerging ideas can be shared and debated amongst very large numbers of partcipants in real time, creates the potential for a more diverse and potentially significantly more challenging discussion about a specific issue. This poses real issues for those leading the participation exercise as they seek to maintain 'control' over a social media process where they may:

• not know the true identity of the particpants;

• have little to no direct control over the characteristics of the respondent (respondents have typically self-selected to participate) — the profile of participants may not be representative leading to the realibility, validity and consequently value, of the final feedback being questioned;

• not know to what extent seemingly separate responses have in fact been submitted by the same individual (e.g. under aliases);

- set ground rules on what types of comments are not acceptable but beyond this have very limited ability to influence the actual content of the responses;

- subsequently discover that a number of responses are identical and could have been orchestrated.

Given all of the above, there are considerable challenges in terms of preserving the reputation of the organisation(s) involved in the participation exercise, when specific issues are opened up for widespread debate under these conditions.

So, given these risks, you might ask, "Should we avoid using social media in participation altogether?"

The answer is probably "no" because the reality is, if you don't use them, there is the distinct possibility that others, who wish to debate the issues on their terms, will initiate a debate of their own on your topic. In this scenario, your level of control and influence will be even less.

These dynamics and their attendant challenges are not a feature of the other methods we have described. Consequently, using social media merits specific consideration.

WHY WOULD I CHOOSE TO USE SOCIAL MEDIA?

So let's sum up, what is distinctive about social media and its influence on a participation process compared with other methods?

The fundamental issue is this - the ease and speed with which large sets of knowledge and opinions can be shared amongst those leading the participation exercise and, significantly, the participants themselves is very different from the other methods.

The prevalence of social media and the increasing familiarity of citizens with these tools presents both major opportunities and challenges for those wishing to engage in user participation.

The key question is not whether social media has a role in participation but rather what role would be meaningful within any particular exercise.

What's important about what you have just read?

There are a variety of methods you can use – based on your understanding of what's involved and the relative strengths and weaknesses of each approach, consider carefully what methods would be most appropriate for your participation exercise i.e. quantitative, qualitative, mixed methods and/or emerging methods.

The individual methods differ in lots of ways – therefore, think carefully about what are the most appropriate and cost-effective ways of engaging your stakeholders, particularly your key stakeholders.

Plan your participation approach carefully – be mindful of the time and budget you have to work within and, then within this, ask yourself, who are the most important groups to be consulted? What specifically do they need to be asked? Be clear on how you will seek to maximise their participation Itemise the specific skills and equipment that will you deploy in order for your participation exercise to be effective. Finally, be clear on how you will pilot your preferred approach(es).

5.0
AFTER USER PARTICIPATION

THE MOST ROBUST INTERPRETATIONS OF DATA EMERGE WHEN PEOPLE ARE ENCOURAGED TO CHALLENGE ONE ANOTHER'S VIEWS.

In this chapter we will explore how to go about:
• Analysing the findings and testing the robustness of the findings;
• Figuring out what the findings 'mean'; and,
• Recording the findings and feeding back to the various individuals, organisations and groupings that contributed and/are impacted by the findings and conclusions of your participation exercise.

5.1 ANALYSING THE FINDINGS
'Analysis' is concerned with the mechanical process of studying a set of data, either notes of interviews or focus groups, or statistics collected via a survey, so as to determine what issues are being raised, how often and by whom.

5.2 Understanding the meaning behind the facts and figures

In the preceding chapter, we described various ways that you could go about analysing the data you collect from particular methods of participation. For example, interviews and focus groups typically lend themselves to content analysis. Survey data, meanwhile, lends itself to statistical analysis using either specialised software or spreadsheets. This analysis of individual datasets is the first level of analysis.

A further level of analysis, often called 'triangulation', is the comparison of the results from two or more methods that were used to capture data on a particular topic(s). The reasoning behind this is that you can be more confident about a result if different methods produce the similar findings.

WHY IS THAT IMPORTANT?

Well, if you used only one method to examine specific topics during your participation exercise, you, and others, may be tempted to simply accept the results you get at face value i.e. without really questioning them. However, this could be misleading because it is possible that had you deployed two methods to examine the same topic(s), you may have discovered that the results differed. Similarly, it may have been that by using three methods to explore a particular topic it could have emerged that two out of the three methods produced similar answers, or if three differing findings emerge, you and others will be aware that the topic under examination is more complex than it seemed and needs to be further reframed and the methods of investigation reconsidered, or both.

In all of your analysis, you are doing two things. We will refer to these two things as the 'vertical' run through the data and the 'horizontal' run through the data. Essentially, you are 'weaving' data sets together and, in doing so, you are making comparisons between them and, at the same time, you are making judgements about the salience of the various themes identified.

In the 'vertical run through' the data, you are going through each data set, one by one, and relating what you have found to each of the original terms of reference for your participation exercise, again one by one, simply noting the findings and the trends.

In the 'horizontal' run through, you are looking at all of the findings pertaining to a particular aspect of the terms of reference together. In effect, you are examining a cluster of data – different types and textures – and it is your challenge to make sense of this. In doing this, it may seem to you that all of the data you have captured is congruent and seems to point in a specific direction in terms of the development of a particular product or service.

However, it is not unusual for some datasets to suggest that a product or service is developed in one particular way and for the other data sets to offer no view on this or to suggest something completely different.

"In all of your analysis, you are doing two things. We will refer to these two things as the 'vertical' run through the data and the 'horizontal' run through the data. Essentially, you are 'weaving' data sets together and, in doing so, you are making comparisons between them and, at the same time, you are making judgements about the salience of the various themes identified."

This is where interpretation and judgement come in. You will need to judge (and there is no single right way to do this) which findings from what data sets are the most important in the context of your participation exercise.

Whilst no one can provide you with a formula for doing this, the best guidance we can offer you is to work with your steering group, and others in order to:

• Be clear on the views of your key stakeholders;

• Compare this with the strength and prevalence of the views of those who could sabotage an attempt to go in the direction suggested by the views of your key stakeholders; and,

• Consider what way(s) forward is/are likely to meet with the greatest level of support from/be of greatest benefit to the greatest number of key

stakeholders. Be sure to involve the steering group in these deliberations and actively welcome all challenges to the interpretation of the results.

The very process of challenge and critical review – which often lends itself to a workshop session - will increase the likelihood that any final interpretation will be more robust.

5.3
RECORDING THE FINDINGS AND FEEDING BACK

It is a core principle of good participation to feedback to those who contribute. Whatever the format for the feedback, the underlying goal is to summarise and share information in relation to the following three aspects:

WHAT WE ASKED
i.e. The terms of reference for the participation exercise and the various questions/types of questions that various stakeholders were asked;

WHAT THE VARIOUS CONSTITUENCIES SAID
The key findings from the participation exercise, highlighting where there was general agreement of various issues and where opinions differed;

WHAT WE DID
A summary of the main actions that have been taken/will be taken as a direct consequence of the feedback received during the participation exercise.

As part of this process, it is important to share with those who took part the rationale for any of their key suggestions not being taken up.

The actual format and medium that you finally choose to record and subsequently feedback the findings, conclusions and recommendations from the participation exercise could vary depending on your target audience(s) and the formats and mediums in which they prefer to receive information.

Another factor will be your overall budget and you may have to prioritise which formats to select.

For some audiences, (e.g. academics), the preferred format could be a highly technical-style report detailing, for example, the methods used, the limitations, the findings, the processes used to analyse the data and the results obtained with further detail on the reliability and validity of these results.

Other audiences e.g. business community and/or community groups, may simply want to have an outline of the methodology (without the technical details), and summary information on the key findings, conclusions and recommendations.

Some audiences will prefer a hard copy written report. Others may be happy to receive information by e-copy and/or to download it from a web site.

Others still may prefer a short summary of the key points by video

or an interactive seminar or workshop where they have an opportunity to ask further questions of those leading the participation exercise. Another option for feeding back the findings is to work in partnership with network-type organisations who are willing disseminate your feedback on the participation exercise on your behalf e.g. on their web site or at their regular meetings.

What's important about what you have just read?

Analysing data sets is done in stages – the first level of analysis is concerned with examining the results from individual data sets.

Judgement is needed to interpret the data – there is no simple formula to describe the process one needs to go through to make sense of clusters of data.

The most robust interpretations of different data sets emerge when, in an atmosphere of trust and respect, a diverse group of individuals feel free to, and are encouraged to challenge one another's views.

The way in which you record and present you findings will vary – be mindful of the difference preferences of your target audiences and, as best you can within your budget, prepare and deliver a report and/or presentation of the results of your participation exercise in a style that suits their needs/preferences.

6.0
GOVERNANCE
& ETHICS

GOVERNANCE FRAMEWORKS AND ETHICAL FRAMEWORKS VARY.
YOU WILL HAVE TO CREATE FRAMEWORKS THAT SUIT YOUR NEEDS.

In this chapter we will highlight:
· Key points about how participation exercises are governed;
· Key ethical considerations when conducting participation exercises.

6.1 GOVERNANCE
6.1.1 WHAT IS GOVERNANCE?
'Governance' refers to a set of rules, regulations, principles and standards of good practice that have been specifically designed to achieve, and continuously improve, the quality of participation work.

6.1.2 WHY DO WE NEED GOVERNANCE?

Governance is needed in order to:

· Ensure that there are sufficient safe guards in place to protect those contributing to a participation exercise and those carrying it out, to thereby minimise the risk of any party being harmed by the participation exercise;

· Ensure the roles and responsibilities of each party are clear and understood;

· Improve the ethical and scientific quality of the participation exercise;

· Monitor the conduct of the work and its effectiveness;

· Promote proactive and constructive review of the exercise so as to assist with the identification of good practice and ensure that any lessons are actually learned.

6.1.3
WHAT SORTS OF THINGS ARE COVERED IN A GOVERNANCE FRAMEWORK?

The precise format for a governance framework will differ depending on the context and the amount of detail required. Any regulatory or guidance system needs to be appropriate to the level of risk to participants and researchers.

For example, a participation exercise involving only healthy, resilient, confident people, for example, should require fewer constraints than a one involving vulnerable people e.g. frail, older people, people with mental health problems, cancer patients etc.

Notwithstanding this, the following sections are fairly typical:

DEFINITIONS AND INTERPRETATIONS
covering aspects such as:

- Who (person or organisation) is leading the participation exercise and taking overall responsibility for it;

- Who is funding the work (if applicable);

- Who is the key contact within the party(ies) responsible for carrying out the participation exercise (sometimes referred to as the 'Lead Investigator')

- What the participation exercise is about (sometimes referred to as 'the research')

- What data or information will be generated by the research (sometimes referred to as the 'results')

- What is considered to the boundaries of the participation 'project' i.e. the 'research' and the 'results' combined.

> **"A participation exercise involving only healthy, resilient, confident people, for example, should require fewer constraints than one involving vulnerable people e.g. frail, older people, people with mental health problems, etc."**

GENERAL CONDITIONS

This sets out the professional and/or organisational standards/protocols within which the participation exercise will be conducted.

PROTECTING INTEGRITY

Details of how the 'scientific' aspects of the participation exercise will be protected e.g. what provisions are in place if anyone from the team conducting the participation exercise were to fake or willfully misrepresent the findings.

EMPLOYMENT OF STAFF

Describes which organisations (i.e. from amongst those conducting the participation exercise) are actually employing staff as part the exercise.

This is important to clarify because, employers have very specific legal obligations towards employees. Whilst these obligations vary from country to country and can vary depending on the type of employment, the range of provisions typically span issues which have potentially significant financial implications (e.g. salary, insurance , contributions, holiday pay, sick pay, maternity/paternity leave, carers leave, career breaks).

In addition, there is always the potential for claims for compensation at any stage within a participation process. It is therefore essential that organisations are clear from the outset about who they are, and who they are not, employing on the project.

This clarity is especially important when organisations are working in partnership but their individuals members of staff are working as a team on a common participation project. In this scenario, unless there is a clear understanding in advance, there is the potential for confusion over which organisation is legally responsible for which individuals.

FINANCES

This section describes how the lead organisation proposes to deal with a range of financial matters including:

- The payment of salaries to employees. If the participation exercise extends over a considerable period, it would be appropriate to describe how salary reviews would be conducted;

- The payment of general expenses (e.g. travel, advertising etc.);

- The payment of equipment;

- The payment of consumables;

- The cost of auditing; and,

- The payment of any work carried out by sub-contractors (e.g. specialised elements of the participation exercise).

TIMESCALES

This section describes when the participation exercise begins and ends. This is important because in some cases certain tasks (e.g. drawing down funding from various bodies) can only take place within designated time bands. Any over-run on the exercise could therefore have potential financial implications.

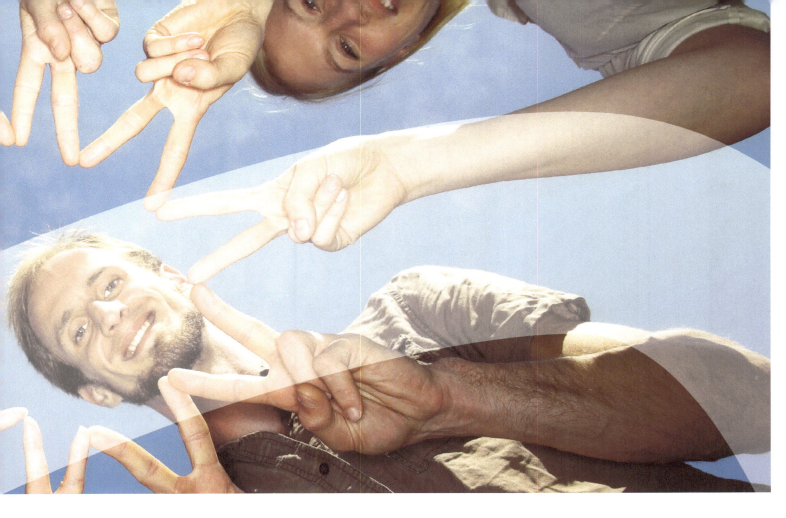

PUBLICITY, PUBLICATION AND DISSEMINATION OF RESULTS

This section describes the lead organisation's requirements in terms of:

- When and how it wishes to be notified if the findings of the research are to be shared with any other party;

- The expectations of those leading the participation exercise in terms of how actively they will promote the findings from it; and,

- The lead organisation's expectations of those leading the participation exercise at an operational level in terms of feeding back to participants both at intervals during the exercise and at the end.

INTELLECTUAL PROPERTY

This section defines who will, and under what conditions, own various aspects of and/or the resultant insight/intelligence emerging from the participation exercise.

This is crucially important if the participation exercise leads to the development of a product or service for which there is the potential for considerable financial gain.
The organisation that holds the intellectual property rights has the prerogative to exploit this opportunity and others do not.

COPYRIGHT

This section defines who will, and under what conditions, own the copyright for various aspects of the participation exercise and/or the final report.
As with intellectual property, this is crucially important if the participation exercise leads to the development of written material for which there is the potential for considerable financial gain.
The organisation that holds the copyright has the prerogative to exploit this opportunity and others do not.

DATA PROTECTION

This describes the obligations of the various organisations involved to agree to observe relevant laws as regards processing and storing personal data.

TERMINATION

The conditions under which the involvement of any party in the participation exercise would be ended prematurely are set out here (e.g. behaviour, relationships with other parties that conflict with the participation exercise in some way and/ or potentially harmful to the reputation of the lead organisation).

APPLICABLE LAW

The legislative context within which any disputes would be processed e.g. the law of England.

ETHICAL CONSIDERATIONS

See next section.

FUTURE TERMS AND CONDITIONS

This typically contains wording that gives the lead organisation the freedom to revise the various clauses in its governance framework as required.

6.2 ETHICS

6.2.1 WHAT ARE ETHICS?
'Ethics' is the name given to a set values and ways of working (essentially a set of principles) which, when taken together, describe how the rights, dignity, safety and well-being of both participants and those leading the participation exercise, will be safeguarded and respected within the exercise.

6.2.2 WHY DO WE NEED ETHICS?

The fundamental purpose of ethics is to protect. The challenge is to review the proposed processes for participation and decide whether it could possibly cause any harm (emotional as well as physical) to the participant.

An ethics committee (which could be part or the same membership as your steering group) should only give approval for the participation exercise when it is satisfied that:

• There are negligible or minimal risks to anyone taking part;

• Those taking part are clear about what is expected of them; and,

• Everyone is aware that they can decline to take part or can withdraw from the participation exercise at any time.

Ethics is the set of principles which has primacy above all others. It assesses what types of participation process(es) are appropriate and which are not.

If a particular part of the participation exercise is judged to be incompatible with the ethical framework, then that part of the participation exercise must be adjusted so that it conforms with the ethical framework, before it can proceed.

If, for whatever reason, a particular aspect cannot be adjusted, then that element which is not compatible with the ethical framework must be dropped from the participation exercise.

"The fundamental purpose of ethics is to protect. The challenge is to review the proposed processes for participation and decide whether it could possibly cause any harm (emotional as well as physical) to the participant."

6.2.3
WHAT SORTS OF THINGS ARE COVERED IN AN ETHICAL FRAMEWORK?

As with the governance framework, the precise format and detail required for an ethical framework will differ depending on the context.

Again, it needs to be appropriate to the level of risk both to participants and researchers. The following sections are fairly typical:

MISSION, AIMS AND VALUES
This sets out the overall goals and value base of the lead organisation and sets the overall context for the specific ethical guidelines that follow.

ETHICAL PRINCIPLES
This will span a range of issues including:

CONSENT
The arrangements for obtaining informed consent from participants.

DATA PROTECTION
The use and protection of personal data.

CONFIDENTIALITY
The mechanisms for ensuring confidentiality of personal information and to the security of those systems.

INVOLVEMENT
The mechanisms to ensure meaningful involvement of participants (and where appropriate, their representative groups) wherever possible, in the design, conduct and reporting of the participation exercise.

RESPECT
The arrangements for assuring respect for the multi-cultural nature and diversity of human society and conditions.

RISK ASSESSMENT
The processes through which any and all risks (physical, emotional or otherwise) to participants and researchers are assessed.

COMPENSATION
The arrangements for explaining the process for compensation to participants in the event of non-negligent harm.

What's important about what you have just read?

Governance issues need to be clarified – these describe not only the overall management arrangements for the project but also clarify and document key roles and responsibilities across the various players. This includes legal and financial obligations.

Ethical issues take primacy overall all else – the goal of ethics is to protect those involved in the participation exercise from harm.

Clarifying the ethical framework at the outset, and referring to it as the participation exercise proceeds, is an integral element of the overall participation exercise. Any aspect of the participation exercise that does not comply with the ethical framework must not be allowed to proceed.

Variations – the format and content of governance frameworks and ethical frameworks differ depending on the nature, scale and complexity of various projects. Whilst many examples of both exist in the public domain, you will ultimately have to create your own frameworks which accurately and completely reflect the needs of your own participation exercise.

7.0
KEY POINTS FOR PARTICIPATION

PUTTING IT ALL TOGETHER AND REFLECTING ON WHAT YOU HAVE ACCOMPLISHED.

• Key points about how participation exercises are carried out;
• Key considerations when conducting participation exercises.

In this final chapter we shall reflect on the key points for user participation. We will look at what is important before, during and after participation. We will also look at governance and ethics.

7.1 BEFORE USER PARTICIPATION

DYNAMISM
User participation is a dynamic, multi-faceted process.

STRUCTURE
Participation exercises always have a beginning, a middle and an end.

PRINCIPLES
There are a set of key principles which, when observed, greatly enhance the quality and effectiveness of participation exercises.

DO THE PRIORITISING OF STAKEHOLDERS WITH OTHERS
There are usually different views on who really holds 'power' or is 'interested'. These debates in themselves yield useful insights which are hugely beneficial to any participation exercise.

INVEST THE MAJORITY OF YOUR TIME AND RESOURCES IN INVOLVING THE 'KEY PLAYERS'
i.e. those stakeholders with the greatest level of power and interest.

AGAIN, LOOK AT THE BEST PRACTICE PRINCIPLES AND ASK YOURSELF, 'WHICH OF THESE IS MOST IMPORTANT TO THE 'KEY PLAYERS'
Make sure you have defined appropriate indicators of success that relate to these principles and that you have a strong evidence cluster i.e., evidence of 'success' being collected via different methods from different parts of the participation exercise.

7.2
DURING USER PARTICIPATION
There are a variety of methods you can use – based on your understanding of what's involved and the relative strengths and weaknesses of each approach, consider carefully what methods would be most appropriate for your participation exercise i.e. quantitative, qualitative, mixed methods and/or emerging methods.

The individual methods differ in lots of ways – therefore, think carefully about what are the most appropriate and cost-effective ways of engaging your stakeholders, particularly your key stakeholders.

As outlined earlier, plan your participation approach carefully – be mindful of the time and budget you have to work within and, then within this, ask yourself, who are the most important groups to be consulted?

Be clear on how you will seek to maximise their participation. Itemise the specific skills and equipment that will you deploy in order for your participation exercise to be effective. Finally, be clear on how you will pilot your preferred approach.

7.3
AFTER USER PARTICIPATION

ANALYSING DATA SETS IS DONE IN STAGES
The first level of analysis is concerned with examining the results from individual date sets.

JUDGEMENT IS NEEDED TO INTERPRET THE DATA
There is no simple formula to describe the process one needs to go through to make sense of clusters of data. The most robust interpretations of different data sets emerge when, in an atmosphere of trust and respect,

a diverse group of individuals feel free to, and are encouraged to, challenge one another's views.

THE WAY IN WHICH YOU RECORD AND PRESENT YOU FINDINGS WILL VARY
Be mindful of the difference preferences of your target audiences and, as best you can within your budget, prepare and deliver a report and/or presentation of the results of your participation exercise in a style that suits their needs/preferences.

7.4
GOVERNANCE AND ETHICS

GOVERNANCE ISSUES NEED TO BE CLARIFIED
These describe not only the overall management arrangements for the project but also clarify and document key roles and responsibilities across the various players. This includes legal and financial obligations.

ETHICAL ISSUES TAKE PRIMACY OVERALL ALL ELSE
The goal of ethics is to protect those involved in the participation exercise from harm.

Clarifying the ethical framework at the outset, and referring to it as the participation exercise proceeds, is an integral element of the overall participation exercise.

Any aspect of the participation exercise that does not comply with the ethical framework must not be allowed to proceed.

VARIATIONS
The format and content of governance frameworks and ethical frameworks differ depending on the nature, scale and complexity of various projects.

Whilst many examples of both exist in the public domain, you will ultimately have to create your own frameworks which accurately and completely reflect the needs of your own participation exercise.

"The individual methods differ in lots of ways – Therefore, think carefully about what are the most appropriate and cost-effective ways of engaging your stakeholders, particularly your key stakeholders.

Plan your participation approach carefully – Be mindful of the time and budget you have to work within and, then within this, ask yourself, who are the most important groups to be consulted? What specifically do they need to be asked?"

APPENDIX

CASE STUDY

ACKNOWLEDGEMENT
The authors wish to extend their thanks to Edinburgh City Council
for allowing us to draw on the key features and findings of an
actual participation exercise that was carried out on behalf of the
Council by Social Market Research in partnership with the Social
Research Centre in 2009.

In order to illustrate the full range of learning points within
this Toolkit, some sections below have been added and others
modified. Notwithstanding this, the example below illustrates
the processes of agreeing the aims of the participation exercise,
identifying the stakeholders, making choices about the
appropriate techniques for involvement, analysing the findings,
drawing conclusions, sharing the findings and then, finally, taking
practical action on the insights that have been obtained.

Listening to citizens about their needs and expectations in relation to the council's community recycling centres (CRCs)

BEFORE USER PARTICIPATION

WHAT IS THE BACKGROUND?

Lead Organisation: Local Council

Key information about the CRCs:
At the time of participation exercise, the arrangements regarding the CRCs within the Council area were as follows.

The Council had four community recycling centres – North, South, East and West.

A variety of materials could be deposited at CRCs (e.g. car batteries, cardboard, electric and electronic equipment etc)

Reuse cabins were provided onsite for the donation of reusable household items (operated by a local charity)

There was little evidence available of how the four centres are currently used or what customers think about them.

In 2008, satisfaction with city-wide recycling services was recorded at 74% which represented an increase of 10 percentage points on the 64% recorded in 2007. It is noted that these satisfaction levels related to all recycling services and not specifically to CRCs.

Satisfaction with city-wide recycling services varied by area, with the highest level of satisfaction recorded in the West (84%) and the lowest among City Centre residents (53%).

RATIONALE -
WHY ARE WE DOING THIS?

Governance: An internal Steering Group was established which comprised a small number of senior staff from the Council's research division and two staff from Technical Services. This Steering Group deliberated and clarified the purpose of the participation exercise.

Purpose: The overall purpose was agreed to be:

"To assess the attitudes and behaviour of existing and potential service users and their needs and expectations of the service in relation to the Council's Community Recycling Centres (CRCs)"

Ethics: The Steering Committee considered the nature and gravity of any risk to both participants and those carrying out the participation exercise. No significant risks were identified and hence no ethical issues were highlighted.

Partners : An independent social policy research company was appointed to gather the necessary data, analyse it and report back.

WHO NEEDS TO PARTICIPATE?

The Council identified that it wishes to obtain views from users and potential users of the CRCs. These could be regarded as the 'external' stakeholders'. The relationship with existing users was considered to be strong and positive because these individuals are in contact with Council staff at the CRCs on a regular basis. In contrast, the relationship with potential users was considered to be weak – i.e. no recent contact with Council staff at the CRCs

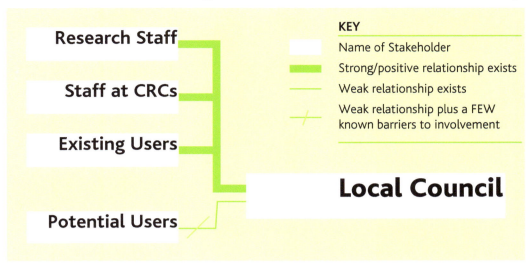

KEY

☐	Name of Stakeholder
━━━	Strong/positive relationship exists
───	Weak relationship exists
─┼─	Weak relationship plus a FEW known barriers to involvement

Research Staff

Staff at CRCs

Existing Users

Potential Users

Local Council

plus the Council was not clear on how best to motivate such individuals to use the facilities (hence the barrier).

The other stakeholders were 'internal' – the research staff – who were effectively commissioning the participation exercise and the staff at the CRC's who would be impacted in some way by the findings. In terms of 'power' and 'interest', existing users were considered to be 'high' on both. In contrast, potential users were rated low on 'interest' but high on 'power' on that basis that whilst they were not currently using the CRC's, they could make a significant contribution to the recycling targets if they could be motivated to do so. In a sense, their 'power' may have been latent, but no less real.

As regards, the internal stakeholders, the research staff were considered to have a high level of 'power' and 'interest' because they could determine the boundaries of the exercise. Likewise, albeit in a different way, the staff at the CRCs were deemed to have a high level of power and interest

because, a) their co-operation was necessary for the conduct of the research ('power') and b) the results would impact on them directly or indirectly ('interest').

WHAT DOES 'SUCCESS' LOOK LIKE?

The Steering Group deliberated on what would make for an effective participation exercise and indicated that the independent research company that was carrying out the participation exercise on its behalf should generate data and insight on the following issues:

• Customer needs and reasons underlying use of the community recycling centres (a clear understanding of these needs is necessary to design an appropriate service);

• Customer experience – ease of use, staff attitudes, customer care (past and present experience of using community recycling centres, as this is likely to influence their future expectations);

• Customer satisfaction and expectations of service (since expectations play a central role in influencing satisfaction);

• Attitudes and motivation of potential customers, the reasons why they do not currently use the community recycling facilities; and,

• Suggested areas for improvement and increasing attractiveness of recycling; and,

• How best to communicate with customers.

All of this was important because the outcomes of the participation exercise were to be used to:

• Inform customer communications and marketing;

• Develop a more customer focused service; and,

• Report customer feedback to staff, customers and potential customers and senior management with the Council.

DURING PARTICIPATION

Types of user participation selected:

The research company that was appointed was mindful of the time (3 months) and budget constraints (less than £10k GBP) of the exercise. Consequently, in partnership with the Steering Group, methods were selected which:

• Maximised participation from each of the stakeholder groups;
• Yielded high levels of insight; and,
• Were feasible to deploy in the time and budget available.

SURVEY OF EXISTING USERS

• 900 achieved interviews (Interview duration 10 mins)

• Interviews conducted face-to-face, on site (at CRCs)

• Representative sample of users achieved from each of the four sites

• Sampling methodology reflected the different user volumes for each site.

• All sites were surveyed on all days of the week.

• Interviewers applied a random selection procedure.

• Survey was piloted, refined and rolled out.

FOCUS GROUPS WITH POTENTIAL USERS

• 31 participants – 14 male; 17 female;

• All four CRC areas represented;

• Mix of gender, ages and social classes;

• Use of Electronic Audience Response System.

A survey was used to capitalise on the accessibility of the existing users.

A face-to-face method, at each of the CRCs, whilst more expensive than some of the alternatives, was favoured because it was more interactive and had the potential to yield richer insights.

In addition, it allowed for greater control over the characteristics of the sample (i.e. as compared with an online survey).

On deciding on an appropriate sample size a number of factors came into consideration.

First it was important to have a sufficient number of cases to ensure that data on user experience is both statistically valid and reliable.

A second consideration was to ensure a sufficient number of cases to allow an analysis of user perception across the four sites.

Given these factors, a target of at least 800 interviews was set. It was also important to ensure that the sampling methodology reflected the different user volumes for each site.

It was agreed that focus groups, supplemented with the use of an electronic audience response system, would be the most appropriate tools to explore the issues that potential users wished to raise.

Online methods would have been considerably more complex and less likely to have delivered the rich interaction that live focus groups do.

The recruitment for the focus groups was designed so that there was a balance of views from male and female, different age groups and different social classes. The focus groups were hosted in a local, neutral venue.

"It was agreed that focus groups, supplemented with the use of an electronic audience response system, would be the most appropriate tools to explore the issues that potential users wished to raise. Online methods would have been considerably more complex and less likely to have delivered the rich interaction that live focus groups do."

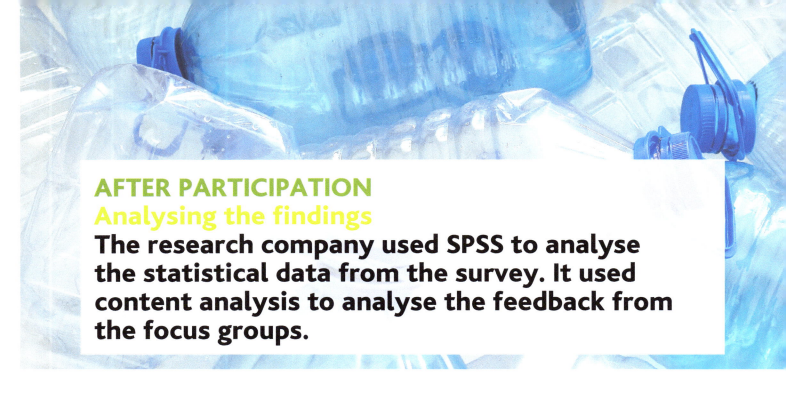

AFTER PARTICIPATION
Analysing the findings
The research company used SPSS to analyse the statistical data from the survey. It used content analysis to analyse the feedback from the focus groups.

It then revisited each of the issues that were to be examined – one by one – and summarised its key findings based on the available information. The issues to be examined and the results are set out below.

WHAT HAVE BEEN THE CUSTOMER NEEDS AND REASONS UNDERLYING THE USE OF COMMUNITY RECYCLING CENTRES (A CLEAR UNDERSTANDING OF THESE NEEDS IS NECESSARY TO DESIGN AN APPROPRIATE SERVICE)?

• Users of CRCs are disproportionately from social classes ABC1 (77%), male (71%) with an average age of 49;

• Almost half (48%) of customers having been using CRCs for more than 5 years;

• Most customers are using CRCs for general recycling (45%) or as part of a home 'clear out' (43%), with almost all (98%) finding the CRCs easy to get to;

• 69% of current customers travelled 3 miles or less to get to a CRC with those living in the East of the City travelling shorter distances;

• Customers were more likely to be aware of the Seafield CRC (78%) and least likely to be aware of Sighthill (54%);

• 61% had used a CRC in the previous month, with residents in the West of the City more likely to use CRCs at least monthly (74%);

• Living near CRCs (48%) and 'word of mouth' (46%) were the most common ways in which users had found out about CRCs;

Self-reported understanding of what can and cannot be recycled at CRCs was high, with 93% of users rating their understanding as either 'excellent' (27%) or 'good' (66%);

• Recycling cardboard (45%) and glass bottles (27%) were the most common reasons for using CRCs;

WHAT HAS BEEN THE CUSTOMER EXPERIENCE – EASE OF USE, STAFF ATTITUDES, CUSTOMER CARE (PAST AND PRESENT EXPERIENCE OF USING COMMUNITY RECYCLING CENTRES, AS THIS IS LIKELY TO INFLUENCE THEIR FUTURE EXPECTATIONS)?;

CURRENT USERS

• 99% of customers are satisfied with the range of materials which can be recycled at CRCs;

• Recycling plastic/plastic bags and paints were the items most likely to be cited by customers when asked what other materials they should be able to recycle;

• User satisfaction with all aspects of service provision at CRCs was high, ranging from 100% satisfaction with layout, cleanliness, personal safety, through to signage to get to CRCs (94%);

• Customer safety and being able to recycle a good range of materials were identified as the aspects of service most important to customers;

• Ensuring customer safety and ease of access were the aspects of service which the service scored highest in terms of performance;

- 90% of customers have had contact with CRC staff, with staff achieving satisfaction ('excellent or good') ratings of 95%+ on politeness, friendliness, willingness to lend a hand, professionalism, providing advice and helpfulness;

POTENTIAL USERS

Some of the potential users had limited experience of the CRCs and some of this had been negative. For example, the following types of concerns were raised:

- Difficulties actually accessing the CRCs – having to cross a dual carriage way to gain entry;

- Staff at CRCs not always as helpful as they could be. Frustration at not been offered assistance when it seemed to the potential user that they needed help.

- Some had been turned away because they had arrived in a van and CRC staff assumed they were commercial and not residential users and refused entry;

- Some felt they had to wait too long in a queue to get materials unloaded;

- A few found them time-consuming to use because when they got to the CRC it was not clear to them what the procedure was i.e. what went where etc.

HOW SATISFIED OR DISSATISFIED ARE CUSTOMERS WITH THE CURRENT SERVICE AND WHAT ARE THEIR EXPECTATIONS OF IT?

CURRENT USERS

- All customers (100%) were satisfied with the service provided by CRCs;

- 99% of CRC users said they would recommend CRCs to a friend;

POTENTIAL USERS

Potential users appeared to desire a recycling service that:

- was convenient;

- made little or no demand on their personal time;

- was low mess or mess-free;

- was low cost or no cost to them;

- gave them a real incentive to recycle – (either intellectual/emotional or financial); and,

- where they could be assured that the materials were actually being recycled (i.e. and not simply going to landfill).

ATTITUDES AND MOTIVATION OF POTENTIAL CUSTOMERS; THE REASONS WHY THEY DO NOT CURRENTLY USE THE COMMUNITY RECYCLING FACILITIES

The main reasons cited by potential customers for non-use were:

- Inconvenience (10 out 32 potential users cited this as their main reason) – Comments from participants highlighted time consuming nature of recycling, need to make a special journey to get there, 'hassle', 'too much trouble' especially if no access to transport.

- No need (7 out of 32 participants) – kerbside collection was already meeting needs of around one fifth of the focus group participants.

There was a general expectation that the Council should be doing more to make it easy to recycle particularly in relation to assisting citizens to actually get their recycling to the CRC.

The lack of transport was a key issue for some. Enhancing public transport was suggested almost as a theoretical solution.

It was clear from the comments that there was little appetite to use public transport to port bulky, and potentially messy recycling materials from one place to another. This was simply perceived as too burdensome.

WHAT DO THE FINDINGS MEAN?

Taking all of the above into consideration, and taking on board the following suggestions for improvements and increasing attractiveness, it was clear that:

• A range of practical measures would be needed to increase the likelihood of greater usage of the CRCs; and,

• A fresh message needed to be developed and communicated to both amongst users and non-users to increase the use of the CRCs. Whilst the available data suggested that different channels of communication might be preferred by users and potential users respectively a wider study of potential users would be needed to confirm this.

Suggested areas for improvement and increasing attractiveness of recycling (use of CRCs specifically)

The following suggestions need to viewed in the context against the backdrop of generally positive attitudes towards recycling (100% satisfaction with the CRC service). Also close to two thirds of potential users indicated that they held a 'positive' or very positive' view towards the concept).

KEY SUGGESTIONS

The key suggestions made by current users were:

• Improved opening hours was the most commonly suggested improvement, albeit by only 11 customers in the survey;

• More advertising (46%) was identified as the main factor which would encourage greater use of the CRC service, with heavier fines for fly tipping suggested by 19% of customers;

• 30% of customers had heard of or seen Council communications in relation specifically to CRCs, with leaflets (66%) and posters (30%) the most commonly mentioned materials;

• 91% of customers exposed to Council communications said that they had done something positive in relation to recycling i.e. thought about recycling, actually recycled, talked about recycling, used a CRC or found out more about recycling.

• Increase awareness of CRCs and other recycling facilities/services across the city;

• Provide free transport to take materials to the CRC (either as part of ordinary collection or special collections)

• Make it more convenient – Reduce or eliminate the perceived 'hassle' with sorting and storing what were perceived as 'messy' and bulky recycling materials.

• Create an incentive – For example, an intellectual / emotional incentive by explaining what happens to the materials and how valuable these materials are; or some kind of financial incentive – cash or 'points' for waste scheme was suggested.

• Provide more help at the CRCs for people requiring assistance e.g. unloading materials.

• Involve children and young people via their schools. Promote the concept of recycling.

• Improve the integration of kerb side collection schemes with CRCs – It was not clear to potential users why CRCs accepted the same materials as can be disposed of by kerb side collection. Need to explain the rationale for what seemed like a 'dual' system.

HOW TO BEST COMMUNICATE WITH CUSTOMERS

TERMINOLOGY

The term 'Community Recycling Centre' does not appear to be in widespread use amongst the potential users consulted. Alternative names, with negative connotations, such as 'the dump', 'the tip' featured much more often. This suggests more needs to be done to encourage the widespread use of the term 'Community Recycling Centre' and, in so doing, create positive associations with CRCs.

METHODS OF COMMUNICATION

CURRENT USERS

• 24% would like to receive information on the service provided by CRCs, with 48% suggesting that this information should be made available via leaflets. The Council website was suggested by 18% of users with the same number suggesting local newspapers.

POTENTIAL USERS

• Radio and leaflets - the focus group participants (potential users) indicated that 'radio' (8 out of 32) and 'leaflets' (7 out of 32) were their top two preferences in terms of how best the Council could communicate with them regarding CRCs.

• The Council Magazine was not the preferred method, none of the focus group participants identified the 'Council magazine' or 'posters' as their perceived 'best' method.

• Social Networking - the younger participants (16 – 25 year olds) were the only focus group that suggested using social networking as a mode of communication. Older participants (25+) seemed to prefer more traditional methods, TV, radio, paper-based etc.

Potential users also made several suggestions for improvement in relation to the current leaflet on CRCs. The points made spanned:

• Use of a tick sheet – to denote facilities at each CRC;

• Improvements to the visual impact (e.g. photos);

• Quality and durability;

• Structure – key points need to be highlighted; less words, more diagrams;

• Text size – needs to be larger

• 'City map' of all recycling facilities requested;

• Colour scheme – Desire for softer colour scheme, with request for green as the dominant colour;

• Size – suggested a larger leaflet would be necessary;

• Key information – variety of key information to be included;

• Recycled paper – need to use recycled paper to print the leaflet.

KEY INFORMATION / MESSAGES

POTENTIAL USERS

The focus group participants identified the following as being the three most important information items to them:

• The opening times (26 out of 94 preferences expressed);

• What is accepted (20 out of 94 preferences expressed); and,

• The locations (19 out of 94 preferences expressed).

However, the analysis of the feedback shows that a variety of other information was also thought to be necessary, including:

• Logistics and process

• Who's who

• Help available

• What happens to the material? (A key issue)

• Justification/benefits of recycling – (i.e. 'Why bother?')

• Where to get recycled materials

• Help line details

• Financial aspects

• Bus links

• Rationale for the different recycling schemes/services

• Future plans for recycling in the city.

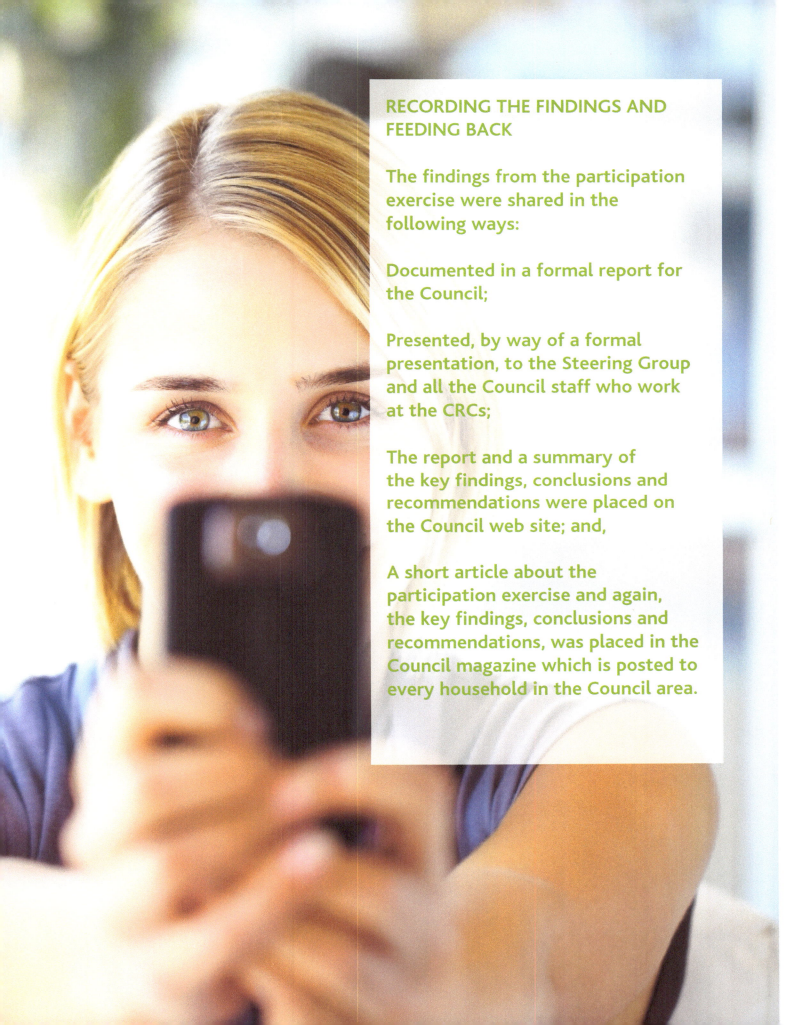

RECORDING THE FINDINGS AND FEEDING BACK

The findings from the participation exercise were shared in the following ways:

Documented in a formal report for the Council;

Presented, by way of a formal presentation, to the Steering Group and all the Council staff who work at the CRCs;

The report and a summary of the key findings, conclusions and recommendations were placed on the Council web site; and,

A short article about the participation exercise and again, the key findings, conclusions and recommendations, was placed in the Council magazine which is posted to every household in the Council area.

NOTES SECTION

NOTES SECTION

ISBN 978-1-85923-247-7
ISBN 978-1-85923-247-7 (ebook)